The Chakras

THE CROWN CHAKRA

The Chakras

C. W. Leadbeater

*This publication made possible with
the assistance of the Kern Foundation*

The Theosophical Publishing House
Wheaton, Ill. U.S.A.
Madras, India/London, England

ISBN: 0-8356-0422-5
Library of Congress Catalog Card Number: 73-147976

Printed in the United States of America

PUBLISHER'S NOTE

IN preparing this edition for publication, a few explanatory footnotes have been added and a few sentences have been omitted which were relevant only at the time of the original publication. Except for minor editorial corrections, the book appears in the same form as when it was first published in 1927.

PREFACE TO THE FIRST EDITION

WHEN a man begins to develop his senses, so that he may see a little more than everybody sees, a new and most fascinating world opens before him, and the chakras are among the first objects in that world to attract his attention. His fellow-men present themselves under a fresh aspect; he perceives much with regard to them which was previously hidden from his eyes, and he is therefore able to understand, to appreciate and (when necessary) to help them much better than he could before. Their thoughts and feelings are expressed clearly before his eyes in colour and form; the stage of their development, the condition of their health become obvious facts instead of mere matters of inference. The brilliant colouring and the rapid and incessant movement of the chakras bring them immediately under his observation, and he naturally wants to know what they are and what they mean. It is the object of this book to provide an answer to those questions and to give to those who have not yet made any attempt to unfold their dormant faculties some idea of at least this one small section of what is seen by their more fortunate brethren.

In order to clear away inevitable preliminary misconceptions, let it be definitely understood that there is nothing fanciful or unnatural about the sight which enables some men to perceive more than others. It is simply an extension of faculties with which we are all familiar, and to acquire it is to make oneself sensitive to vibrations more rapid than those to which our physical senses are normally trained to respond. These faculties will come to everyone in due course of evolution, but some of us have taken special trouble to develop them now in advance of the rest, at the cost of many years of harder work than most people would care to undertake.

I know that there are still many men in the world who are so far behind the times as to deny the existence of such powers, just as there are still villagers who have never seen a railway train. I have neither time nor space to argue with such invincible ignorance; I can only refer enquirers to my book on *Clairvoyance*,[1] or to scores of books by other authors on the same subject. The whole case has been proved hundreds of times, and no one who is capable of weighing the value of evidence can any longer be in doubt.

Much has been written about the chakras, but it is chiefly in Sanskrit or in some of the Indian vernaculars. It is only quite recently that any account of them has appeared in English. I mentioned them myself in *The Inner Life*[1] about 1910, and since then Sir John Woodroffe's magnificent work *The Serpent Power*[1] has been issued, and some of the other Indian books have been translated. The symbolical drawings

[1] The Theosophical Publishing House.

of them which are used by the Indian yogis were
reproduced in *The Serpent Power*, but so far as I am
aware the illustrations which I give in this book are
the first attempt to represent them as they actually
appear to those who can see them. Indeed, it is
chiefly in order to put before the public this fine
series of drawings by my friend the Rev. Edward
Warner that I write this book, and I wish to express
my deep indebtedness to him for all the time and
trouble that he has devoted to them. I have also to
thank my indefatigable collaborator, Professor Ernest
Wood, for the collection and collation of all the
valuable information as to the Indian views on our
subject which is contained in Chapter V.

Being much occupied with other work, it was
my intention merely to collect and reprint as accompanying letterpress to the illustrations the various
articles which I had long ago written on the subject;
but as I looked over them certain questions suggested
themselves and a little investigation put me in possession
of additional facts, which I have duly incorporated.
An interesting point is that both the vitality-globule
and the kundalini-ring were observed by Dr. Annie
Besant and catalogued as hyper-meta-proto elements
as long ago as 1895, though we did not then follow
them far enough to discover their relation to one
another and the important part that they play in the
economy of human life.

1927   C. W. L.

CONTENTS

CHAPTER IV

THE DEVELOPMENT OF THE CHAKRAS

CHAPTER V

THE LAYA YOGA

LIST OF ILLUSTRATIONS

PLATES

FIGURES

TABLES

CHAPTER I

THE FORCE-CENTRES

THE MEANING OF THE WORD

THE word Chakra is Sanskrit, and signifies a wheel. It is also used in various subsidiary, derivative and symbolical senses, just as is its English equivalent; as we might speak of the wheel of fate, so does the Buddhist speak of the wheel of life and death; and he describes that first great sermon in which the Lord Buddha propounded his doctrine as the *Dhammachakkappavattana Sutta* (*chakka* being the Pali equivalent for the Sanskrit *chakra*) which Professor Rhys Davids poetically renders as " to set rolling the royal chariot-wheel of a universal empire of truth and righteousness ". That is exactly the spirit of the meaning which the expression conveys to the Buddhist devotee, though the literal translation of the bare words is " the turning of the wheel of the Law ". The special use of the word chakra with which we are at the moment concerned is its application to a series of wheel-like vortices which exist in the surface of the etheric double of man.

Preliminary Explanations

As this book may probably fall into the hands of some who are not familiar with Theosophical terminology it may be well to insert here a few words of preliminary explanation.

In ordinary superficial conversation a man sometimes mentions his soul—implying that the body through which he speaks is the real man, and that this thing called the soul is a possession or appanage of that body—a sort of captive balloon floating over him, and in some vague sort of way attached to him. This is a loose, inaccurate and misleading statement; the exact opposite is the truth. Man *is* a soul and owns a body—several bodies in fact; for besides the visible vehicle by means of which he transacts his business with his lower world, he has others which are not visible to ordinary sight, by means of which he deals with the emotional and mental worlds. With those, however, we are not for the moment concerned.

In the course of the last century enormous advances have been made in our knowledge of the minute details of the physical body; students of medicine are now familiar with its bewildering complexities, and have at least a general idea of the way in which its amazingly intricate machinery works.

The Etheric Double

Naturally, however, they have had to confine their attention to that part of the body which is dense enough to be visible to the eye, and most of them are probably unaware of the existence of that type of matter, still physical though invisible, to which in Theosophy we give the name of etheric.* This invisible part of the physical body is of great importance to us, for it is the vehicle through which flow the streams of vitality which keep the body alive, and without it as a bridge to convey undulations of thought and feeling from the astral to the visible denser physical matter, the ego † could make no use of the cells of his brain. It is clearly visible to the clairvoyant as a mass of faintly-luminous violet-grey mist, interpenetrating the denser part of the body, and extending very slightly beyond it.

The life of the physical body is one of perpetual change, and in order that it shall live it needs constantly to be supplied from three distinct sources. It must have food for its digestion, air for its breathing, and vitality in three forms for its absorption. This vitality is essentially a force, but when clothed with matter it appears to us as though it were a highly-refined chemical element. It exists upon all planes, but our business for the moment is to consider its manifestation in the physical world.

In order to understand that, we must know something of the constitution and arrangement of this etheric part of our bodies. I have written on this

* Not to be confused with " aether " which some consider to be the medium for electro-magnetic waves. (Ed.)

† Individuality, not to be confused with the use of the term in psychology. (Ed.)

subject many years ago in various volumes, and
Colonel A. E. Powell has recently gathered together
all the information heretofore published * and issued
it in a convenient form in a book called *The Etheric
Double.*†

THE CENTRES

The chakras or force-centres are points of connection at which energy flows from one vehicle or
body of a man to another. Anyone who possesses
a slight degree of clairvoyance may easily see them
in the etheric double, where they show themselves
as saucer-like depressions or vortices in its surface.
When quite undeveloped they appear as small circles
about two inches in diameter, glowing dully in the
ordinary man; but when awakened and vivified they
are seen as blazing, coruscating whirlpools, much
increased in size, and resembling miniature suns.
We sometimes speak of them as roughly corresponding
to certain physical organs; in reality they show themselves at the surface of the etheric double, which projects
slightly beyond the outline of the dense body. If we
imagine ourselves to be looking straight down into
the bell of a flower of the convolvulus type, we shall
get some idea of the general appearance of a chakra.
The stalk of the flower in each springs from a point
in the spine, so another view might show the spine
as a central stem (see Plate VIII), from which flowers

* 1925
† The Theosophical Publishing House.

shoot forth at intervals, showing the opening of their bells at the surface of the etheric body.

The seven centres with which we are at present concerned are indicated in the accompanying illustration (Fig. 1). Table I gives their English and Sanskrit names.

All these wheels are perpetually rotating, and into the hub or open mouth of each a force from the higher world is always flowing—a manifestation of the life-stream issuing from the Second Aspect of the Solar Logos—which we call the primary force. That force is sevenfold in its nature, and all its forms operate in each of these centres, although one of them in each case usually predominates over the others. Without this inrush of energy the physical body could not exist. Therefore the centres are in operation in every one, although in the undeveloped person they are usually in comparatively sluggish motion, just forming the necessary vortex for the force, and no more. In a more evolved man they may be glowing and pulsating with living light, so that an enormously greater amount of energy passes through them, with the result that there are additional faculties and possibilities open to the man.

THE FORM OF THE VORTICES

This divine energy which pours into each centre from without sets up at right angles to itself (that is to say, in the surface of the etheric double) secondary forces in undulatory circular motion, just as a

This shows a man, with chakras all round him.

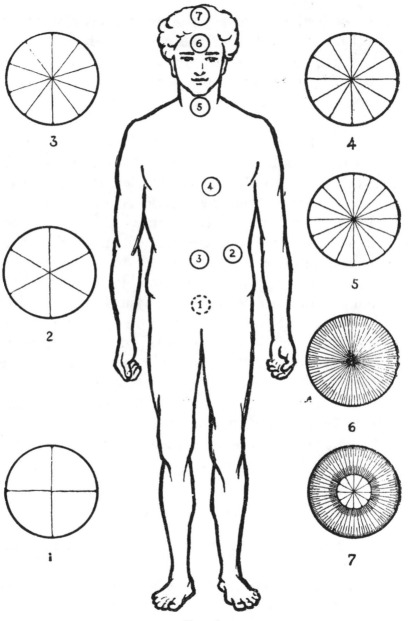

FIG. 1

ENGLISH NAME	SANSKRIT NAME	SITUATION
Root or Basic Chakra	Mūlādhāra	At the base of the spine
Spleen or Splenic Chakra	*	Over the spleen
Navel or Umbilical Chakra	Manipūra	At the navel, over the solar plexus
Heart or Cardiac Chakra	Anāhata	Over the heart
Throat or Laryngeal Chakra	Vishuddha	At the front of the throat
Brow or Frontal Chakra	Ājnā	In the space between the eyebrows
Crown or Coronal Chakra	Sahasrāra	On the top of the head

TABLE I

bar-magnet thrust into an induction coil produces a current of electricity which flows round the coil at right angles to the axis or direction of the magnet. The primary force itself, having entered the vortex, radiates from it again at right angles, but in straight lines, as though the centre of the vortex were the hub of a wheel, and the radiations of the primary force its spokes. By means of these spokes the force seems to bind the astral and etheric bodies together as though with grappling-hooks. The number of these spokes

* The spleen chakra is not indicated in the Indian books; its place is taken by a centre called the *Svādhishthāna*, situated in the neighbourhood of the generative organs, to which the same six petals are assigned. From our point of view the arousing of such a centre would be regarded as a misfortune, as there are serious dangers connected with it. In the Egyptian scheme of development elaborate precautions were taken to prevent any such awakening. (See *The Hidden Life in Freemasonry*.)

differs in the different force-centres, and determines the number of waves or petals which each of them exhibits. Because of this these centres have often been poetically described in Oriental books as resembling flowers.

Each of the secondary forces which sweep round the saucer-like depression has its own characteristic wave-length, just as has light of a certain colour; but instead of moving in a straight line as light does, it moves along relatively large undulations of various sizes, each of which is some multiple of the smaller wave-lengths within it. The number of undulations is determined by the number of spokes in the wheel, and the secondary force weaves itself under and over the radiating currents of the primary force, just as basket-work might be woven round the spokes of a carriage-wheel. The wave-lengths are infinitesimal, and probably thousands of them are included within one of the undulations. As the forces rush round in the vortex, these oscillations of different sizes, crossing one another in this basket-work fashion, produce the flower-like form to which I have referred. It is, perhaps, still more like the appearance of certain saucers or shallow vases of wavy iridescent glass, such as are made in Venice. All of these undulations or petals have that shimmering pavonine effect, like mother-of-pearl, yet each of them has usually its own predominant colour, as will be seen from our illustrations. This nacreous silvery aspect is likened in Sanskrit works to the gleam of moonlight on water.

THE ILLUSTRATIONS

These illustrations of ours show the chakras as seen by clairvoyant sight in a fairly evolved and intelligent person, who has already brought them to some extent into working order. Of course our colours are not sufficiently luminous—no earthly colours could be; but at least the drawings will give some idea of the actual appearance of these wheels of light. It will be understood from what has already been said that the centres vary in size and in brightness in different people, and that even in the same person some of them may be much more developed than the rest. They are drawn about life-size, except for the Sahasrāra or crown chakra, which we have found it necessary to magnify in order to show its amazing wealth of detail. In the case of a man who excels greatly in the qualities which express themselves through a certain centre, that centre will be not only much enlarged but also especially radiant, throwing out brilliant golden rays. An example of that may be seen in Madame Blavatsky's precipitation of the aura of Mr. Stainton Moses, which is now kept in a cabinet in the archives of the Society at Adyar. It is reproduced, though very imperfectly, on page 364 of Volume I of Colonel Olcott's *Old Diary Leaves*.

These chakras naturally divide into three groups, the lower, the middle and the higher; they might be called respectively the physiological, the personal and the spiritual.

The first and second chakras, having but few spokes or petals, are principally concerned with receiving into the body two forces which come into it at that physical level—one being the serpent-fire from the earth and the other the vitality from the sun. The centres of the middle group, numbered 3, 4 and 5, are engaged with the forces which reach man through his personality—through the lower astral in the case of centre 3, the higher astral in centre 4, and from the lower mind in centre 5. All these centres seem to feed certain ganglia in the body. Centres 6 and 7 stand apart from the rest, being connected with the pituitary body and the pineal gland respectively, and coming into action only when a certain amount of spiritual development has taken place.

I have heard it suggested that each of the different petals of these force-centres represents a moral quality, and that the development of that quality brings the centre into activity. For example, in *The Dhyāna-bindu Upanishad*, the petals of the heart chakra are associated with devotion, laziness, anger, charity and similar qualities. I have not yet met with any facts which definitely confirm this, and it is not easy to see exactly how it can be, because the appearance is produced by certain readily recognizable forces, and the petals in any particular centre are either active or not active according as these forces have or have not been aroused, and their unfoldment seems to have no more direct connection with morality than has the enlargement of the biceps. I have certainly met with persons in whom some of the centres were in full activity, though the moral advancement was by no means exceptionally high, whereas in other persons of high spirituality and the noblest possible morality the centres were scarcely yet vitalized at all; so that there does not seem to be any necessary connection between the two developments.

There are, however, certain facts observable which may be the basis of this rather curious idea. Although the likeness to petals is caused by the same forces flowing round and round the centre, alternately over and under the various spokes, those spokes differ in character, because the inrushing force is subdivided into its component parts or qualities, and therefore each spoke radiates a specialized influence of its own, even though the variations be slight. The secondary force, in passing each spoke, is to some extent modified by its influence, and therefore changes a little in its hue. Some of these shades of colour may indicate a form of the force which is helpful to the growth of some moral quality, and when that quality is strengthened its corresponding vibration will be more pronounced. Thus the deepening or weakening of the tint might be taken to betoken the possession of more or less of that attribute.

THE ROOT CHAKRA

The first centre, the basic (Plate I), at the base of the spine, has a primary force which radiates out in four spokes, and therefore arranges its undulations so as to give the effect of its being divided into quadrants, alternately red and orange in hue, with hollows between them. This makes it seem as though marked with the sign of the cross, and for that reason the cross is often used to symbolize this centre, and sometimes a flaming cross is taken to indicate the serpent-fire which resides in it. When acting with any vigour this chakra is fiery orange-red in colour, corresponding closely with the type of vitality which is sent down to it from the splenic centre. Indeed, it will be noticed that in the case of every one of the chakras a similar correspondence with the colour of its vitality may be seen.

THE SPLEEN CHAKRA

The second centre, the splenic (Plate II), at the spleen, is devoted to the specialization, subdivision and dispersion of the vitality which comes to us from the sun. That vitality is poured out again from it in six horizontal streams, the seventh variety being drawn into the hub of the wheel. This centre therefore has six petals or undulations, all of different colours, and is specially radiant, glowing and sunlike. Each of the six divisions of the wheel shows predominantly the colour of one of the forms of the vital force—red, orange, yellow, green, blue and violet.

THE NAVEL CHAKRA

The third centre, the umbilical (Plate IV), at the navel or solar plexus, receives a primary force with ten radiations, so it vibrates in such a manner as to divide itself into ten undulations or petals. It is very closely as ociated with feelings and emotions of various kinds. Its predominant colour is a curious blending of several shades of red, though there is also a great deal of green in it. The divisions are alternately chiefly red and chiefly green.

THE HEART CHAKRA

The fourth centre, the cardiac (Plate V), at the heart, is of a glowing golden colour, and each of its quadrants is divided into three parts, which gives it twelve undulations, because its primary force makes for it twelve spokes.

THE THROAT CHAKRA

The fifth centre, the laryngeal (Plate VII), at the throat, has sixteen spokes, and therefore sixteen apparent divisions. There is a good deal of blue in it, but its general effect is silvery and gleaming, with a kind of suggestion as of moonlight upon rippling water. Blue and green predominate alternately in its sections.

THE BROW CHAKRA

The sixth centre, the frontal (Plate IX), between the eyebrows, has the appearance of being divided into halves, one chiefly rose-coloured, though with a great deal of yellow about it, and the other predominantly a kind of purplish-blue, again closely agreeing with the colours of the special types of vitality that vivify it. Perhaps it is for this reason that this centre is mentioned in Indian books as having only two petals, though if we are to count undulations of the same character as those of the previous centres we shall find that each half is subdivided into forty-eight of these, making ninety-six in all, because its primary force has that number of radiations.

This sudden leap form 16 to 96 spokes, and again the even more startling variation from 96 to 972 between this and the next chakra, show us that we are now dealing with centres of an altogether different order from those which we have hitherto been considering. We do not yet know all the factors which determine the number of spokes in a chakra, but it is already evident that they represent shades of variation in the primary force. Before we can say much more than this, hundreds of observations and comparisons must be made—made, repeated and verified over and over again. But meantime this much is clear—that while the need of the personality can be satisfied by a limited number of types of force, when we come to the higher and more permanent principles of man we encounter a complexity, a multiplicity, which demands for its expression a vastly greater selection of modifications of the energy.

THE CROWN CHAKRA

The seventh centre, the coronal (see *frontispiece*), at the top of the head, is when stirred into full activity the most resplendent of all, full of indescribable chromatic effects and vibrating with almost inconceivable rapidity. It seems to contain all sorts of prismatic hues, but is on the whole predominantly violet. It is described in Indian books as thousand-petalled, and really this is not very far from the truth, the number of the radiations of its primary force in the outer circle being nine hundred and sixty. Every line of this will be seen faithfully reproduced in our frontispiece, though it is hardly possible to give the effect of the separate petals. In addition to this it has a feature which is possessed by none of the other chakras—a sort of subsidiary central whirlpool of gleaming white flushed with gold in its heart—a minor activity which has twelve undulations of its own.

This chakra is usually the last to be awakened. In the beginning it is the same size as the others, but as the man progresses on the Path of spiritual advancement it increases steadily until it covers almost the whole top of the head. Another peculiarity attends its development. It is at first a depression in the etheric body, as are all the others, because through it, as through them, the divine force flows in from without; but when the man realizes his position as a king of the divine light, dispensing largesse to all around him, this chakra reverses itself, turning as it were inside out; it is no longer a channel of reception but of radiation, no longer a depression but a prominence, standing out from the head as a dome, a veritable crown of glory.

In Oriental pictures and statues of the deities or great men this prominence is often shown. In Fig. 2 it appears on the head of a statue of the Lord Buddha at Borobudur in Java. This is the conventional method of representing it, and in this form it is to be found upon the heads of thousands of images of the Lord Buddha all over the Eastern world. In many cases it will be seen that the two tiers of the Sahasrāra chakra are copied—the larger dome of 960 petals first, and then the smaller dome of 12 rising out of that in turn. The head on the right is that of Brahmā from the Hokké-do of Tōdai-ji, at Nara in Japan (dating from A.D. 749); and it will be seen that the statue is wearing a head-dress fashioned to represent this chakra, though in a form somewhat different from the last, showing the coronet of flames shooting up from it.

It appears also in the Christian symbology, in the crowns worn by the four-and-twenty elders who are for ever casting them down before the throne of God. In the highly developed man this coronal chakra pours out splendour and glory which makes for him a veritable crown; and the meaning of that passage of Scripture is that all that he has gained, all the magnificent karma that he makes, all the wondrous spiritual force that he generates—all *that* he casts perpetually at the feet of the LOGOS to be used in his work. So, over and over again, can he continue to cast down his golden crown, because it continually re-forms as the force wells up from within him.

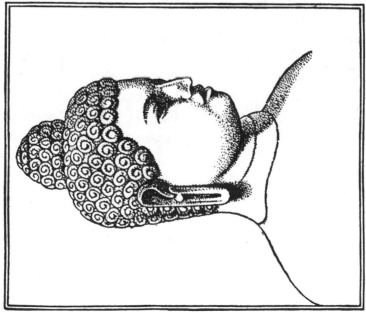

Fig. 2

OTHER ACCOUNTS OF THE CENTRES

These seven force-centres are frequently described in Sanskrit literature, in some of the minor Upanishads, in the Purānas and in Tāntric works. They are used today by many Indian yogis. A friend acquainted with the inner life of India assures me that he knows of one school in that country which makes free use of the chakras—a school which numbers as its pupils about sixteen thousand people scattered over a large area. There is much interesting information available on the subject from Hindu sources, which we will try to summarize with comments in a later chapter.

It appears also that certain European mystics were acquainted with the chakras. Evidence of this occurs in a book entitled *Theosophia Practica* by the well-known German mystic Johann Georg Gichtel, a pupil of Jacob Boehme, who probably belonged to the secret society of the Rosicrucians. It is from this work of Gichtel's that our Plate III is reproduced by the kind permission of the publishers. This book was originally issued in the year 1696, though in the edition of 1736 it is said that the pictures, of which the volume is mainly a description, were printed only some ten years after the death of the author, which took place in 1710. The book must be distinguished from a collection of Gichtel's correspondence put forth under the same title *Theosophia Practica;* the present volume is not in the form of letters, but consists of

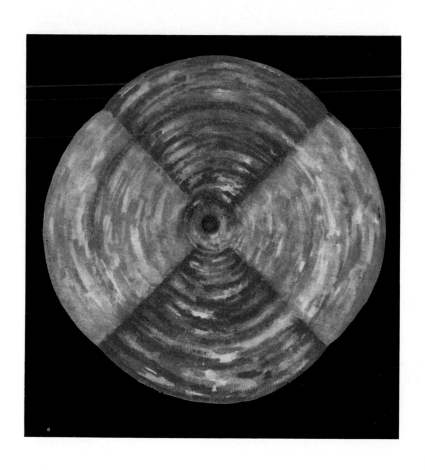

THE ROOT CHAKRA

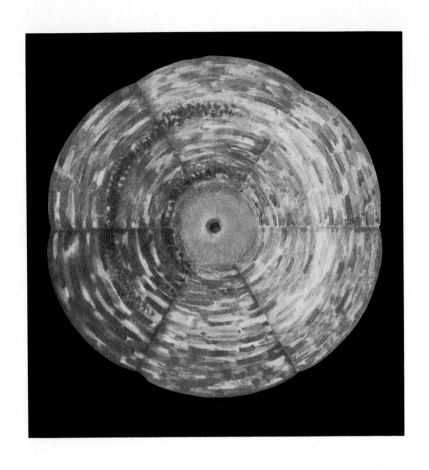

THE SPLEEN CHAKRA

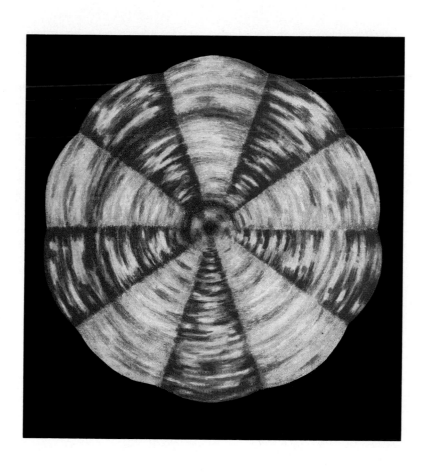

THE NAVEL CHAKRA

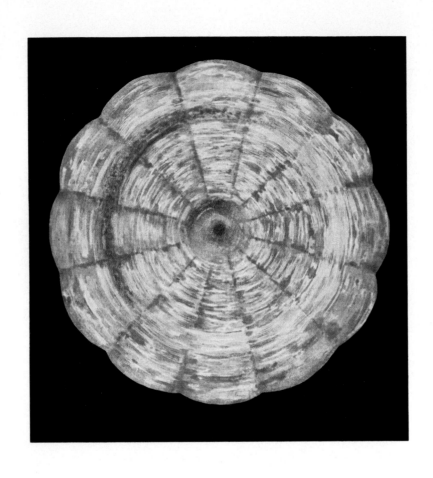

THE HEART CHAKRA

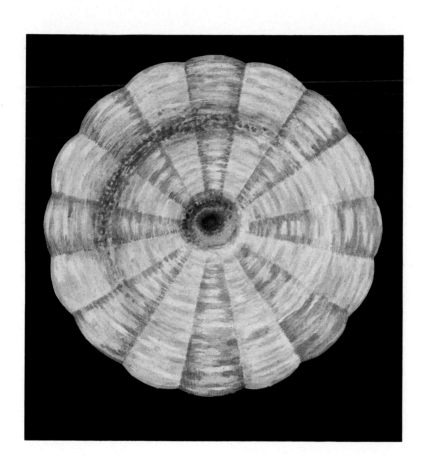

THE THROAT CHAKRA

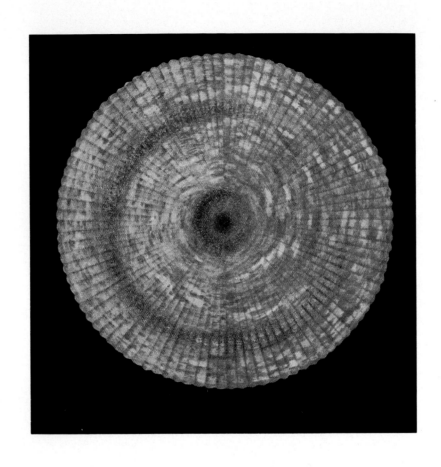

THE BROW CHAKRA

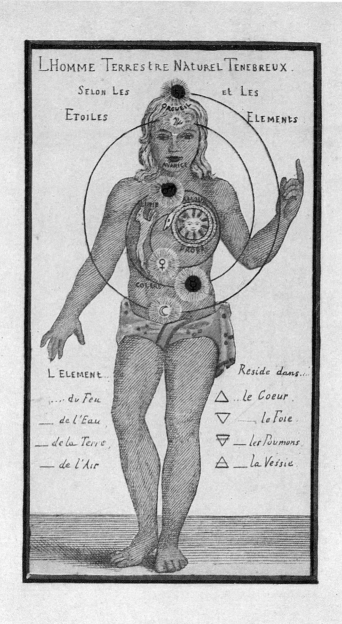

THE CHAKRAS, ACCORDING TO GICHTEL

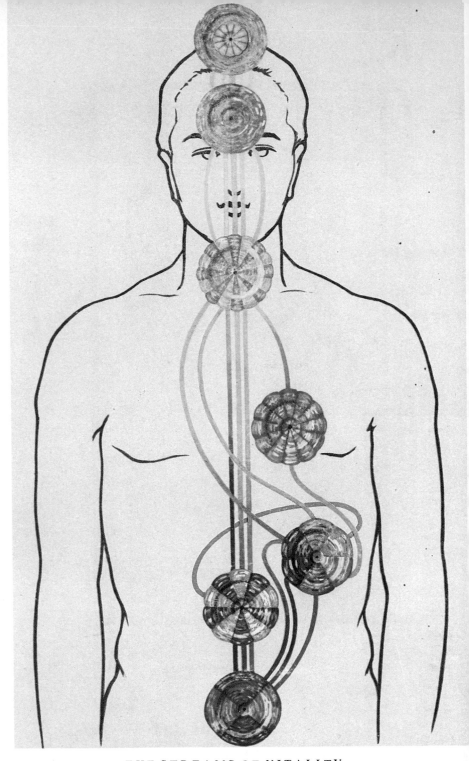

THE STREAMS OF VITALITY

six chapters dealing with the subject of that mystic regeneration which was such an important tenet of the Rosicrucians.

The illustration which we give here has been photographed from the French translation of the *Theosophia Practica*, published in 1897 in the Bibliothèque Rosicrucienne (No. 4) by the Bibliothèque Chacornac, Paris.

Gichtel, who was born in 1638, at Ratisbon in Bavaria, studied theology and law and practised as an advocate; but afterwards, becoming conscious of a spiritual world within, gave up all worldly interests and became the founder of a mystical Christian movement. Being opposed to the ignorant orthodoxy of his time, he drew down upon himself the hatred of those whom he had attacked, and about 1670 he was consequently banished, and his property confiscated. He finally found refuge in Holland, where he lived for the remaining forty years of his life.

He evidently considered the figures printed in his *Theosophia Practica* as being of a secret nature; apparently they were kept within the small circle of his disciples for quite a number of years. They were, he says, the result of an inner illumination—presumably of what in our modern times we should call clairvoyant faculties. On the title-page of his book he says that it is, " A short exposition of the three principles of the three worlds in man, represented in clear pictures, showing how and where they have their respective Centres in the inner man; according to what the author has found in himself in divine contemplation, and what he has felt, tasted and perceived ".

Like most mystics of his day, however, Gichtel lacks the exactitude which should characterize true occultism and mysticism; in his description of the figures he allows himself lengthy, though oftentimes quite interesting digressions on the difficulties and problems of the spiritual life. As an exposition of his illustrations, however, his book is not a success. Perhaps he did not dare to say too much; or he may have wished to induce his readers to learn to see for themselves that of which he was writing. It seems likely that by the truly spiritual life which he led he had developed sufficient clairvoyance to see these chakras, but that he was unaware of their true character and use, so that in his attempts to explain their meaning, he attached to them the current symbolism of the mystic school to which he belonged.

He is here dealing, as will be seen, with the natural earthly man in a state of darkness, so he has perhaps some excuse for being a little pessimistic about his chakras. He lets the first and second pass without comment (possibly knowing that they are chiefly concerned with physiological processes), but labels the solar plexus as the home of anger—as indeed it is. He sees the heart-centre as filled with self-love, the throat with envy and avarice; and the higher centres of the head radiate nothing better than pride.

He also assigns planets to the chakras, giving the Moon to the basic, Mercury to the splenic, Venus to the umbilical, the Sun to the heart (though it will be noted that a snake is coiled round it), Mars to the laryngeal, Jupiter to the frontal, and Saturn to the coronal. He informs us further that fire resides in the heart, water in the liver, earth in the lungs, and air in the bladder.

It is noteworthy that he draws a spiral, starting from the snake round the heart and passing through all the centres in turn; but there seems no very definite reason for the order in which this line touches them. The symbolism of the running dog is not explained, so we are left at liberty to interpret it as we will.

The author gives us later an illustration of the man regenerated by the Christ, who has entirely crushed the serpent, but has replaced the Sun by the Sacred Heart, dripping gore most gruesomely.

The interest of the picture to us, however, is not in the author's interpretations, but in the fact that it shows beyond the possibility of mistake that at least some of the mystics of the seventeenth century knew of the existence and position of the seven centres in the human body.

Further evidence of early knowledge about these force-centres exists in the rituals of Freemasonry, the salient points of which come down to us from time immemorial; the monuments show that these points were known and practised in ancient Egypt, and they have been handed down faithfully to the present day. Masons find them among their secrets, and by utilizing them actually stimulate certain of these centres for the occasion and the purpose of their work, though they generally know little or nothing of what is happening beyond the range of normal sight.   Obviously explanations are impossible here, but I have mentioned as much of the matter as is permissible in *The Hidden Life in Freemasonry*.

CHAPTER II

THE FORCES

THE PRIMARY OR LIFE FORCE

THE Deity sends forth from Himself various forms of energy; there may well be hundreds of which we know nothing; but some few of them have been observed. Each of those seen has its appropriate manifestation at every level which our students have yet reached; but for the moment let us think of them as they show themselves in the physical world. One of them exhibits itself as electricity, another as the serpent-fire, another as vitality, and yet another as the life-force, which is quite a different thing from vitality, as will presently be seen.

Patient and long-continued effort is needed by the student who would trace these forces to their origin and relate them to one another. At the time when I collected into the book *The Hidden Side of Things* the answers to questions which had been asked during previous years at the roof meetings at Adyar, I knew of the manifestation on the physical plane of the life-force, of kundalinī and of vitality, but not yet of their relation to the Three Outpourings, so that

I described them as entirely different and separate from them. Further research has enabled me to fill the gap, and I am glad now to have the opportunity of correcting the mis-statement which I then made.

There are three principal forces flowing through the chakras, and we may consider them as representative of the three aspects of the Logos. The energy which we find rushing into the bell-like mouth of the chakra, and setting up in relation to itself a secondary circular force, is one of the expressions of the Second Out-pouring, from the Second Aspect of the Logos—that stream of life which is sent out by him into the matter already vitalized by the action of the Third Aspect of the Logos in the First Outpouring. It is this which is symbolized when it is said in Christian teaching that the Christ is incarnate of (that is, takes form from) the Holy Ghost and the Virgin Mary.

That Second Outpouring has long ago subdivided itself to an almost infinite degree; not only has it subdivided itself, but it has also differentiated itself—that is to say, it seems to have done so. In reality this is almost certainly only the *māyā* or illusion through which we see it in action. It comes through countless millions of channels, showing itself on every plane and subplane of our system, and yet fundamentally it is one and the same force, in no way for a moment to be confused with that First Outpouring which long ago manufactured the chemical elements from which this Second Outpouring takes the material of which its vehicles at all levels are built. It appears as though some of its manifestations were lower or denser, because it is employing lower and denser matter; on the buddhic level we see it displaying itself as the Christ-principle, gradually expanding and unfolding itself imperceptibly within the soul of the man; in the astral and mental bodies we perceive that various layers of matter are vivified by it, so that we note different exhibitions of it appearing in the higher part of the astral in the guise of a noble emotion, and in the lower part of the very same vehicle as a mere rush of life-force energizing the matter of that body.

We find it in its lowest embodiment drawing round itself a veil of etheric matter, and rushing from the astral body into the flower-like bells of these chakras on the surface of the etheric part of the physical body. Here it meets another force welling up from the interior of the human body—the mysterious power called kundalinī or the serpent-fire.

THE SERPENT-FIRE

This force is the physical-plane manifestation of another of the manifold aspects of the power of the Logos, belonging to the First Outpouring, which comes from the Third Aspect. It exists on all planes of which we know anything; but it is the expression of it in etheric matter with which we have to do at present. It is not convertible into either the primary force already mentioned or the force of vitality which comes from the sun, and it does not seem to be affected in any way by any other forms of physical energy. I have seen as much as a million and a quarter volts of electricity put into a human body, so that when the man held out his arm towards the wall, huge flames rushed out from his fingers, yet he felt nothing unusual, nor would he be in the least burnt under these circumstances unless he actually touched some external object; but even this enormous display of power had no effect whatever upon the serpent-fire.

We have known for many years that there is deep down in the earth what may be described as a laboratory of the Third Logos. On attempting to investigate the conditions at the centre of the earth we find there a vast globe of such tremendous force that we cannot approach it. We can touch only its outer layers; but in doing even that it becomes evident that they are in sympathetic relation with the layers of kundalinī in the human body. Into that centre the force of the Third Logos must have poured ages ago, but it is working there still. There He is engaged in the gradual development of new chemical elements, which show increasing complexity of form, and more and more energetic internal life or activity.

Students of chemistry are familiar with the Periodic Table originated by the Russian chemist Mendeléeff in the latter part of the last century, in which the known chemical elements are arranged in the order of their atomic weights, beginning with the lightest, hydrogen, which has an atomic weight 1, and ending with the heaviest at present known, Uranium, which has a relative weight of 238.5. In our own investigations into these matters we found that these atomic weights were almost exactly proportional to the number of ultimate atoms in each element; we have recorded these numbers in *Occult Chemistry*, and also the form and composition of each element.

In most cases the forms which we found when the elements were examined with etheric sight indicate— as does the Periodic Table also—that the elements have been developed in cyclic order, that they do not lie on a straight line, but on an ascending spiral. We have been told that the elements hydrogen, oxygen and nitrogen (which constitute approximately half the crust of our globe and nearly all its atmosphere) belong at the same time to another and greater solar system, but we understand that the rest of the elements have been developed by the Logos of our system. He is carrying on his spiral beyond uranium, under conditions of temperature and pressure which are quite inconceivable to us. And gradually, as new elements are formed, they are pushed outwards and upwards towards the surface of the earth.

The force of kundalini in our bodies comes from that laboratory of the Holy Ghost deep down in the earth. It belongs to that terrific glowing fire of the underworld. That fire is in striking contrast to the fire of vitality which comes from the sun, which will presently be explained. The latter belongs to air and light and the great open spaces; but the fire which comes from below is much more material, like the fire of red-hot iron, of glowing metal. There is a rather terrible side to this tremendous force; it gives the impression of descending deeper and deeper into matter, of moving slowly but irresistibly onwards, with relentless certainty.

The serpent-fire is not that portion of the energy of the Third Logos with which He is engaged in building denser and denser chemical elements. It is more of the nature of a further development of that force which is in the living centre of such elements as radium. It is part of the action of the life of the Third Logos after it has reached its lowest immersion and is once more ascending towards the heights from which it came. We have long understood that the second life-wave, from the Second Logos, descends into matter through the first, second and third elemental kingdoms, down to the mineral, and then ascends again through the vegetable and animal to the human kingdom, where it meets the downward-reaching power of the First Logos. This is suggested in Fig. 3, in which the oval indicating that Second Outpouring comes down on the left side, reaches its densest point at the bottom of the diagram, and then rises again in the curve on the right-hand side of the figure.

We now find that the force of the Third Logos also rises again after touching its lowest point, so we must imagine that the vertical line in the centre of the figure returns upon its path. Kundalinī is the power of that Outpouring on its path of return, and it works in the bodies of evolving creatures in intimate contact with the primary force already mentioned, the two acting together to bring the creature to the point where it can receive the Outpouring of the First

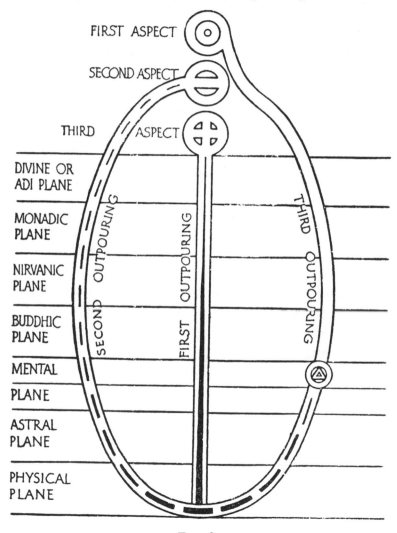

FIG. 3

Logos, and become an ego, a human being, and still carry on the vehicles even after that. We thus draw God's mighty power from the earth beneath as well as from heaven above; we are children of the earth as well as of the sun. These two meet in us, and work together for our evolution. We cannot have one without the other, but if one is greatly in excess there are serious dangers. Hence the risk of any development of the deeper layers of the serpent-fire before the life in the man is pure and refined.

We hear much of this strange fire and of the danger of prematurely arousing it; and much of what we hear is undoubtedly true. There is indeed most serious peril in awakening the higher aspects of this furious energy in a man before he has gained the strength to control it, before he has acquired the purity of life and thought which alone can make it safe for him to unleash potency so tremendous. But kundalini plays a much larger part in daily life than most of us have hitherto supposed; there is a far lower and gentler manifestation of it which is already awake within us all, which is not only innocuous but beneficent, which is doing its appointed work day and night while we are entirely unconscious of its presence and activity. We have of course previously noticed this force as it flows along the nerves, calling it simply nerve-fluid, and not recognizing it for what it really is. The endeavour to analyse it and to trace it back to his source shows us that it enters the human body at the root chakra.

Like all other forces, kundalinī is itself invisible; but in the human body it clothes itself in a curious nest of hollow concentric spheres of astral and etheric matter, one within another, like the balls in a Chinese puzzle. There appear to be seven such concentric spheres resting within the root chakra, in and around the last real cell or hollow of the spine close to the coccyx; but only in the outermost of these spheres is the force active in the ordinary man. In the others it is " sleeping ", as is said in some of the Oriental books; and it is only when the man attempts to arouse the energy latent in those inner layers that the dangerous phenomena of the fire begin to show themselves. The harmless fire of the outer skin of the ball flows up the spinal column, using (so far as investigations have gone up to the present) the three lines of Sushumnā, Idā and Pingalā simultaneously.

THE THREE SPINAL CHANNELS

Of these three currents which flow in and around the spinal cord of every human being Madame Blavatsky writes as follows in *The Secret Doctrine*:

> The Trans-Himālayan school . . . locates *Sushumnā*, the chief seat of these three *Nādīs*, in the central tube of the spinal cord. . . . *Idā* and *Pingalā* are simply the sharps and flats of that *Fa* of human nature, ... which, when struck in a proper way, awakens the sentries on either side, the spiritual Manas and the physical Kāma, and subdues the lower through the higher.*

> It is the pure *Akāsha* that passes up *Sushumnā;* its two aspects flow in *Idā* and *Pingalā*. These are three vital airs, and are

* *The Secret Doctrine*, Fifth Adyar Edition, Vol. V, p. 480.

symbolized by the Brahmanical thread. They are ruled by the
Will. Will and Desire are the higher and lower aspects of one
and the same thing. Hence the importance of the purity of the
canals ... From these three a circulation is set up, and from the
central canal passes into the whole body.*

  Idā and *Pingalā* play along the curved wall of the cord in
which is *Sushumnā*. They are semi-material, positive and negative,
sun and moon, and start into action the free and spiritual current
of *Sushumnā*. They have distinct paths of their own, otherwise
they would radiate all over the body.†

In *The Hidden Life in Freemasonry* I referred to a certain Masonic use of these forces as follows:

  It is part of the plan of Freemasonry to stimulate the activity
of these forces in the human body, in order that evolution may be
quickened. The stimulation is applied at the moment when
R. W. M. creates, receives and constitutes; in the First Degree it
affects the *Idā* or feminine aspect of the force, thus making it easier
for the candidate to control passion and emotion; in the Second
Degree it is the *Pingalā* or masculine aspect which is strengthened,
in order to facilitate the control of mind; but in the Third Degree,
it is the central energy itself, the *Sushumnā*, which is aroused,
thereby opening the way for the influence of the pure spirit from
on high. It is by passing up through this channel of the *Sushumnā*
that a yogi leaves his physical body at will in such a manner that
he can retain full consciousness on higher planes, and bring back
into his physical brain a clear memory of his experiences. The
little figures below give a rough indication of the way in which
these forces flow through the human body; in a man the *Idā* starts
from the base of the spine just on the left of the *Sushumnā* and the
Pingalā on the right (be it understood that I mean the right and
left of the *man*, not the spectator); but in a woman these positions
are reversed. The lines end in the *medulla oblongata*.‡

  The spine is called in India the *Brahmadandā*, the stick of
Brahma; and the drawing given in Fig. 4*d* shows that it is also the
original of the caduceus of Mercury, the two snakes of which
symbolize the *kumdalinī* or serpent-fire which is presently to be
set in motion along those channels, while the wings typify the
power of conscious flight through higher planes which the development of that fire confers. Fig. 4*a* shows the stimulated *Idā* after

* *The Secret Doctrine*, Fifth Adyar Edition, Vol. V, p. 510.
† *Ibid.*, p. 520.
‡ *The Hidden Life in Freemasonry*.

the initiation into the First Degree; this line is crimson in colour. To it is added at the Passing the yellow line of the *Pingalā*, depicted in Fig. 4*b;* while at the Raising the series is completed by the deep blue stream of the *Sushumnā*, illustrated by Fig. 4*c.*

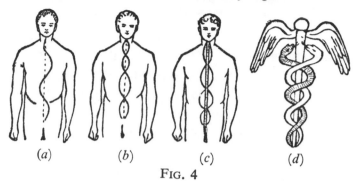

(*a*)   (*b*)   (*c*)   (*d*)

FIG. 4

The kundalinī which normally flows up these is specialized during this upward passage, and that in two ways. There is in it a curious mingling of positive and negative qualities which might almost be described as male and female. On the whole there is a great preponderance of the feminine aspect, which is perhaps the reason why in the Indian books this force is always spoken of as " she ", also perhaps why a certain " chamber in the heart " where kundalinī is centred in some forms of yoga is described in *The Voice of the Silence* as the home of the World's Mother. But when this serpent-fire issues from its home in the root chakra and rises up the three channels which we have mentioned it is noteworthy that the section rising through the channel Pingalā is almost wholly masculine, whereas that rising through the channel Idā is almost wholly feminine. The larger stream passing up the Sushumnā seems to retain its original proportions.

The second differentiation which takes place during the passage of this force up the spine is that it becomes intensely impregnated with the personality of the man. It seems to enter at the bottom as a very general force, and to issue forth at the top as definitely this particular man's nerve-fluid carrying with it the impress of his special qualities and idiosyncrasies, which manifest themselves in the vibrations of those spine-centres which may be considered as the roots from which spring the stems of the surface chakras.

THE MARRIAGE OF THE FORCES

Though the mouth of the flower-like bell of the chakra is on the surface of the etheric body, the stem of the trumpet-like blossom always springs from a centre in the spinal cord. It is almost always to these centres in the spine, and not to the superficial manifestations of them, that the Hindu books refer when they speak of the chakras. In each case an etheric stem, usually curving downwards, connects this root in the spine with the external chakra. (See Plate VI.) As the stems of all the chakras thus start from the spinal cord, this force naturally flows down those stems into the flower-bells, where it meets the incoming stream of the divine life, and the pressure set up by that encounter causes the radiation of the mingled forces horizontally along the spokes of the chakra.

The surfaces of the streams of the primary force and the kundalini grind together at this point, as they revolve in opposite directions and considerable pressure is caused. This has been symbolized as the "marriage" of the divine life, which is vividly male, to the kundalini, which is always considered as distinctively feminine, and the compound energy which results is what is commonly called the personal magnetism of the man; it then vivifies the plexuses which are seen in the neighbourhood of several of the chakras; it flows along all the nerves of the body, and is principally responsible for keeping up its temperature. It sweeps along with it the vitality which has been absorbed and specialized by the spleen chakra.

When the two forces combine as mentioned above there is a certain interlocking of some of the respective molecules. The primary force seems capable of occupying several different kinds of etheric form; that which it most commonly adopts is an octahedron, made of four atoms * arranged in a square, with one central atom constantly vibrating up and down through the middle of the quadrilateral and at right angles to it. It also sometimes uses an exceedingly active little molecule consisting of three atoms. The kundalini usually clothes itself in a flat ring of seven atoms, while the vitality globule, which also consists of seven atoms, arranges them on a plan not unlike that of the primary force, except that it forms a hexagon

---

* The term "atom" used here and throughout the remainder of the book refers not to a chemical atom but to the basic type of matter in the highest sub-plane of each plane of nature. Similarly, "molecule" refers to a grouping of such "atoms' in a way similar to that by which chemical atoms form chemical molecules. (Ed.)

instead of a square. Fig. 5 may help the reader to image these arrangements.

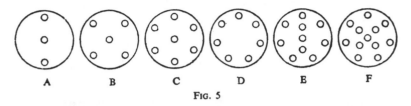

Fig. 5

A and B are forms adopted by the primary force, C is that taken by the vitality globule, and D that of the kundalinī. E shows the effect of the combination of A and D; F that of B and D. In A, B and C the central atom is all the time in rapid vibration at right angles to the surface of the paper, springing up from it to a height greater than the diameter of the disc, and then sinking below the paper to an equal distance, but repeating this shuttle-like motion several times in a second. (Of course it will be understood that I speak relatively and not literally; in reality the sphere which our disc represents is so tiny as to be invisible to the most powerful microscope; but *in proportion* to that size its vibration is as I describe.) In D the only motion is a steady procession round and round the circle, but there is an immense amount of latent energy there which manifests itself as soon as the combinations take place which we have endeavoured to illustrate in E and F. The two positive atoms in A and B continue when thus combined their previous violent activities—in fact, their vigour is greatly intensified; while the atoms in D, though they still move along the same circular pathway, accelerate their speed so enormously that they cease to be visible as separate atoms and appear as a glowing ring.

The first four molecules depicted above belong to the type to which in *Occult Chemistry* Dr. Besant gives the name of Hyper-meta-proto-elemental matter.* Indeed, they may be identical with some of those which she drew for that book. But E and F, being compounds, must be taken as working upon the next sub-plane, which she calls the super-etheric, and so would be classified as meta-proto matter. Type B is far commoner than type A, and it naturally follows that in the nerve-fluid which is the final result of the confluence we find many more examples of F and E. This nerve-fluid is therefore a stream of various elements, containing specimens of each one of the types shown in Fig. 4—simple and compound, married and single, bachelors, old maids and conjugal couples, all rushing onward together.

The marvellously energetic upward and downward movement of the central atom in the combinations E and F gives them a quite unusual shape within their magnetic fields, as shown in Fig. 6.

The upper half of this seems to me to bear a remarkable resemblance to the linga which is frequently to be seen in front of the temples of Shiva in India. I am told that the linga is an emblem of creative power, and that Indian devotees regard it as extending downwards into the earth to just the same extent as it rises

* *Op. cit.*, (Second Edition) p. 25; (Third Edition, 1951) p. 25.

above it. I have wondered whether the ancient Hindus knew of this especially active molecule, and of the immense importance of the part it plays in the support of human and animal life; and whether they carved their symbol in stone as a record of their occult knowledge.

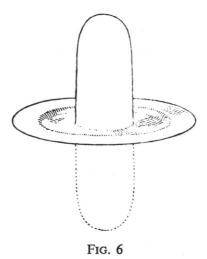

FIG. 6

THE SYMPATHETIC SYSTEM

Anatomists describe two nervous systems in the human body—the cerebro-spinal and the sympathetic. The cerebro-spinal begins with the brain, continues down the spinal cord, and ramifies to all parts of the body through the ganglia from which nerves issue between every two successive vertebræ. The sympathetic system consists of two cords which run almost the whole length of the spine, situated a little forward of its axis, and to the right and left respectively. From the ganglia of these two cords, which are not quite as numerous as those of the spinal cord, sympathetic nerves proceed to form the network systems called the plexuses, from which in turn, as from relay stations, emerge smaller terminal ganglia and nerves. These two systems are, however, interrelated in a great variety of ways by so many connecting nerves that one must not think of them as two distinct neural organizations. In addition we have a third group called the vagus nerves, which arise in the medulla oblongata, and descend independently far into the body, mingling constantly with the nerves and plexuses of the other systems.

The spinal cord, the left sympathetic cord, and the left vagus nerve are all shown in Plate VI. It exhibits the nervous connections between the spinal and sympathetic ganglia, and the channels by which the latter give forth nerves to form the principal plexuses of the sympathetic system. It will be noted that there is a tendency for the plexuses to droop from the ganglia in which they have their origin, so that, for example, the cœliac or solar plexus depends largely upon the great splanchnic nerve, shown in our plate as rising from the fifth thoracic sympathetic ganglion, which in turn is connected with the fourth thoracic spinal ganglion. This is almost on a level with the heart horizontally, but the nerve descends and joins the smaller and the smallest splanchnic nerves, which merge from lower thoracic ganglia, and these pass through the diaphragm and go to the solar plexus.

There are also other connections between that plexus and the cords, shown in the Plate to some extent, but too complicated to describe. The principal nerves leading to the cardiac plexus bend downwards in a similar manner. In the case of the pharyngeal plexus there is but a slight droop, and the carotid plexus even rises upward from the internal carotid nerve, coming from the superior cervical sympathetic ganglion.

THE CENTERS IN THE SPINE

There is a somewhat similar droop in the etheric stem which connects the flowers or chakras on the surface of the etheric double with their corresponding centres in the spine, which are situated approximately in the positions shown in red on Plate VI, and detailed in Table II. The radiating spokes of the chakras supply force to these sympathetic plexuses to assist them in their relay work; in the present state of our knowledge it seems to me rash to identify the chakras with the plexuses, as some writers appear to have done.

The hypogastric or pelvic plexuses are no doubt connected in some way with the Svādhisthāna chakra situated near the generative organs, which is mentioned in Indian books but not used in our scheme of development. The plexuses grouped together in this region are probably largely subordinate to the solar plexus in all matters of conscious activity, as both they and the splenic plexus are connected very closely with it by numerous nerves.

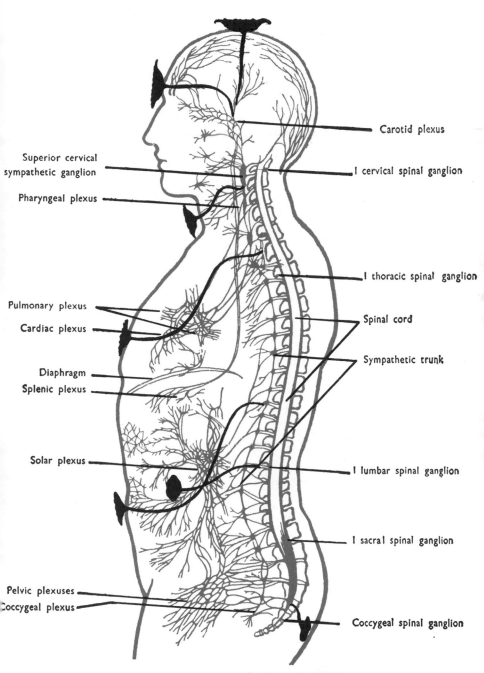

Carotid plexus

Superior cervical sympathetic ganglion

I cervical spinal ganglion

Pharyngeal plexus

I thoracic spinal ganglion

Pulmonary plexus

Cardiac plexus

Spinal cord

Diaphragm

Sympathetic trunk

Splenic plexus

Solar plexus

I lumbar spinal ganglion

I sacral spinal ganglion

Pelvic plexuses

Coccygeal plexus

Coccygeal spinal ganglion

THE CHAKRAS AND THE NERVOUS SYSTEM

Name of Chakra	Position on Surface	Approximate Position of Spinal Chakra	Sympathetic Plexus	Chief Subsidiary Plexuses
Root	Base of spine	4th Sacral	Coccygeal	...
Spleen	Over the spleen	1st Lumbar	Splenic	...
Navel	Over the navel	8th Thoracic	Cœliac or Solar	Hepatic, pyloric, gastric, mesenteric, etc.
Heart	Over the heart	8th Cervical	Cardiac	Pulmonary, coronary, etc.
Throat	At the throat	3rd Cervical	Pharyngeal	...
Brow	On the brow	1st Cervical	Carotid	Cavernous, and cephalic ganglia generally

TABLE II

The crown chakra is not connected with any of the sympathetic plexuses of the physical body, but is associated with the pineal gland and the pituitary body, as we shall see in Chapter IV. It is related also to the development of the brain and spinal system of nerves.

On the origin and relations of the sympathetic and cerebro-spinal systems Dr. Annie Besant writes as follows in *A Study in Consciousness:*

Let us see how the building of the nervous system, by vibratory impulses from the astral, begins and is carried on. We find a minute group of nerve cells and tiny processes connecting

them. This is formed by the action of a centre which has previously appeared in the astral body—an aggregation of astral
matter arranged to form a centre for receiving and responding to
impulses from outside. From that astral centre vibrations pass
into the etheric body, causing little etheric whirlpools which draw
into themselves particles of denser physical matter, forming at last
a nerve cell, and groups of nerve cells. These physical centres,
receiving vibrations from the outer world, send impulses back to
the astral centres, increasing their vibrations; thus the physical and
the astral centres act and re-act on each other, and each becomes
more complicated and more effective. As we pass up the animal
kingdom, we find the physical nervous system constantly improving,
and becoming a more and more dominant factor in the body, and
this first-formed system becomes, in the vertebrates, the sympathetic
system, controlling and energising the vital organs—the heart,
the lungs, the digestive tract; beside it slowly develops the cerebro-
spinal system, closely connected in its lower workings with the
sympathetic, and becoming gradually more and more dominant,
while it also becomes in its most important development the normal
organ for the expression of the " waking-consciousness ". This
cerebro-spinal system is built up by impulses originating in the
mental, not in the astral plane, and is only indirectly related to
the astral through the sympathetic system, built up from the
astral.*

VITALITY

We all know the feeling of cheerfulness and well-
being which sunlight brings to us, but only students
of occultism are fully aware of the reasons for that
sensation. Just as the sun floods his system with
light and heat, so does he perpetually pour out into
it another force as yet unsuspected by modern science
—a force to which has been given the name " vitality ".
This is radiated on all levels, and manifests itself in
each realm—physical, emotional, mental and the rest
—but we are specially concerned for the moment

* *Op. cit.*, pp. 104-5.

with its appearance in the lowest, where it enters some of the physical atoms, immensely increases their activity, and makes them animated and glowing.

We must not confuse this force with electricity, though it in some ways resembles it, for its action differs in many ways from that of either electricity, light or heat. Any of the variants of this latter force cause oscillation of the atom as a whole—an oscillation the size of which is enormous as compared with that of the atom; but this other force which we call vitality comes to the atom not from without, but from within.

THE VITALITY GLOBULE

The atom is itself nothing but the manifestation of a force; the Solar Deity wills a certain shape which we call an ultimate physical atom (Fig. 7), and by

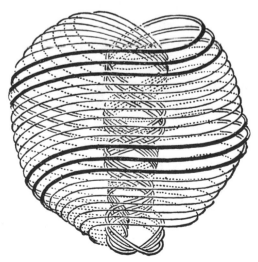

FIG. 7

that effort of His will some fourteen thousand million " bubbles in Koilon " are held in that particular form. It is necessary to emphasize the fact that the cohesion of the bubbles in that form is entirely dependent upon that effort of will, so that if that were for a single instant withdrawn, the bubbles must fall apart again, and the whole physical realm would simply cease to exist in far less than the period of a flash of lightning. So true is it that the world is nothing but illusion, even from this point of view, to say nothing of the fact that the bubbles of which the atom is built are themselves only holes in Koilon, the true æther of space.

So it is the will-force of the Solar Deity continually exercised which holds the atom together as such; and when we try to examine the action of that force we see that it does not come into the atom from outside, but wells up within it—which means that it enters it from higher dimensions. The same is true with regard to this other force which we call vitality; it enters the atom from within along with the force that holds that atom together, instead of acting upon it entirely from without, as do those other varieties of force which we call light, heat or electricity.

When vitality wells up thus within an atom it endows it with an additional life, and gives it a power of attraction, so that it immediately draws round it six other atoms, which it arranges in a definite form, thus making a sub-atomic or hyper-meta-proto-element, as I have already explained. But this element differs from all others which have so far been observed, in that the force which creates it and holds it together comes from the First Aspect of the Solar Deity instead of from the Third.

These globules are conspicuous above all others which may be seen floating in the atmosphere, on account of their brilliance and extreme activity—the intensely vivid life which they show. These are probably the fiery lives so often mentioned by Madame Blavatsky, as, for example, in *The Secret Doctrine,* Vol. I, p. 306, where she writes:

> We are taught that every physiological change, . . . nay, life itself, or rather the objective phenomena of life, produced by certain conditions and changes in the tissues of the body, which allow and force life to act in that body—that all this is due to those unseen " Creators " and " Destroyers ", which are called, in such a loose and general way, microbes. It might be supposed that these Fiery Lives and the microbes of Science are identical. This is not true. The Fiery Lives are the seventh and highest sub-division of the plane of matter, and correspond in the individual with the One Life of the Universe, though only on that plane of matter.

While the force that vivifies these globules is quite different from light, it nevertheless seems to depend upon light for its power of manifestation. In brilliant sunshine this vitality is constantly welling up afresh, and the globules are generated with great rapidity and in incredible numbers, but in cloudy weather there is a great diminution in the number of globules formed, and during the night, so far as we have been able to see, the operation is entirely suspended. In the night, therefore, we may be said to be living upon the stock manufactured in the course of previous days, and though it appears practically impossible that it should ever be entirely exhausted, that stock evidently does run low when there is a long succession of cloudy days. The globule, once charged, remains as a sub-atomic element, and is not subject to any change or loss of force unless and until it is absorbed by some living creature.

THE SUPPLY OF GLOBULES

Vitality, like light and heat, is pouring forth from the sun continually, but obstacles frequently arise to prevent the full supply from reaching the earth. In the wintry and melancholy climes miscalled the temperate, it too often happens that for days together the sky is covered by a funeral pall of heavy cloud, and this affects vitality just as it does light; it does not altogether hinder its passage, but sensibly diminishes its amount. Therefore in dull and dark weather vitality runs low, and over all living creatures there comes an instinctive yearning for sunlight.

When vitalized atoms are thus more sparsely scattered, the man in rude health increases his power of absorption, depletes a larger area, and so keeps his strength at the normal level; but invalids and men of small nerve-force, who cannot do this, often suffer severely, and find themselves growing weaker and more irritable without knowing why. For similar reasons vitality is at a lower ebb in the winter than in the summer, for even if the short winter day be sunny, which is rare, we have still to face the long and dreary winter night, during which we must exist upon such vitality as the day has stored in our atmosphere. On the other hand the long summer day, when bright and cloudless, charges the atmosphere so thoroughly with vitality that its short night makes but little difference.

From the study of this question of vitality, the occultist cannot fail to recognize that, quite apart from temperature, sunlight is one of the most important factors in the attainment and preservation of perfect health—a factor for the absence of which nothing else can entirely compensate. Since this vitality is poured forth not only upon the physical world but upon all others as well, it is evident that, when in other respects satisfactory conditions are present, emotion, intellect and spirituality will be at their best under clear skies and with the inestimable aid of the sunlight.

PSYCHIC FORCES

The three forces already mentioned—the primary, the vitality and the kundalini—are not directly connected with man's mental and emotional life, but only with his bodily well-being. But there are also forces entering the chakras which may be described as psychic and spiritual. The first two centres exhibit none of these, but the navel chakra and the others higher in the body are ports of entry for forces which affect human consciousness.

In an article on Thought-Centres in the book *The Inner Life*, I explained that masses of thought are very definite things, occupying a place in space. Thoughts on the same subject and of the same character tend to aggregate; therefore for many subjects there is a thought-centre, a definite space in the atmosphere, and other thoughts about the same matter are attracted to such a centre, and go to increase its size and influence. A thinker may in this way contribute to a centre, but he in turn may be influenced by it; and this is one of the reasons why people think in droves, like sheep. It is much easier for a man of lazy mentality to accept a ready-made thought from someone else than to go through the mental labour of considering the various aspects of a subject and arriving at a decision for himself.

This is true on the mental plane with regard to thought; and, with appropriate modifications, it is true on the astral plane with regard to feeling. Thought flies like lightning through the subtle matter of the mental plane, so the thought of the whole world on a certain subject may easily gather together in one spot, and yet be accessible and attractive to every thinker on that subject. Astral matter, though so far finer than physical, is yet denser than that of the mental plane; the great clouds of " emotion-forms " which are generated in the astral world by strong feelings do not all fly to one world-centre, but they do coalesce with other forms of the same nature in their own neighbourhood, so that enormous and very powerful "blocks" of feeling are floating about almost everywhere, and a man may readily come into contact with them and be influenced by them.

The connection of this matter with our present subject lies in the fact that when such influence is exercised it is through the medium of one or other of the chakras. To illustrate what I mean, let me take the example of a man who is filled with fear. Those who have read the book *Man Visible and Invisible* will remember that the condition of the astral body of such a man is shown in Plate XIV. The vibrations radiated by an astral body in that state will at once attract any fear-clouds that happen to be in the vicinity; if the man can quickly recover himself and master his fear, the clouds will roll back sullenly, but if the fear remains or increases they will discharge their accumulated energy through his umbilical chakra, and his fear may become mad panic in which he altogether loses control of himself, and may rush blindly into any kind of danger. In the same way one who loses his temper attracts clouds of anger, and renders himself liable to an inrush of feeling which will change his indignation into maniacal fury—a condition in which he might commit murder by an irresistible impulse, almost without knowing it. Similarly a man who yields to depression may be swept into a terrible state of permanent melancholia; or one who allows himself to be obsessed by animal desires may become for the time a monster of lust and sensuality, and may under that influence commit

crimes the thought of which will horrify him when he
recovers his reason.

All such undesirable currents reach the man
through the navel chakra. Fortunately there are
other and higher possibilities; for example there are
clouds of affection and of devotion, and he who feels
these noble emotions may receive through his heart
chakra a wonderful enhancement of them, such as is
depicted in *Man Visible and Invisible* in Plates XI
and XII.

The kind of emotion which affects the navel
chakra in the manner before-mentioned is indicated
in Dr. Besant's *A Study in Consciousness*, where she
divides the emotions into two classes, those of love
and those of hate. All those on the side of hate
work in the navel chakra but those on the side of
love operate in the heart. She writes:

> We have seen that desire has two main expressions: desire
> to attract, in order to possess, or again to come into contact with,
> any object which has previously afforded pleasure; desire to repel,
> in order to drive far away, or to avoid contact with, any object
> which has previously inflicted pain. We have seen that attraction
> and repulsion are the two forms of desire, swaying the Self.
>
> Emotion, being desire infused with intellect, inevitably
> shows the same division into two. The emotion which is of the
> nature of attraction, attracting objects to each other by pleasure,
> the integrating energy in the universe, is called love. The emotion
> which is of the nature of repulsion, driving objects apart from each
> other by pain, the disintegrating energy in the universe, is called
> hate. These are the two stems from the root of desire, and all the
> branches of the emotions may be traced back to one of these twain.
>
> Hence the identity of the characteristics of desire and
> emotions; love seeks to draw to itself the attractive object, or to
> go after it, in order to unite with it, to possess, or to be possessed
> by it. It binds by pleasure, by happiness, as desire binds. Its

ties are indeed more lasting, more complicated, are composed of more numerous and more delicate threads interwoven into greater complexity, but the essence of desire-attraction, the binding of two objects together, is the essence of emotion-attraction, of love. And so also does hate seek to drive from itself the repellent object or to flee from it, in order to be apart from it, to repulse, or be, repulsed by it. It separates by pain, by unhappiness. And thus the essence of desire-repulsion, the driving apart of two objects, is the essence of emotion-repulsion, of hate. Love and hate are the elaborated and thought-infused forms of the simple desires to possess and to shun.

Later on, Dr. Besant explains that each of these two great emotions subdivides into three parts, according as the man who has it feels strong or weak.

Love looking downwards is benevolence; love looking upwards is reverence; and these are the several common characteristics of love from superiors to inferiors, and from inferiors to superiors universally. The normal relations between husband and wife, and those between brothers and sisters, afford us the field for studying the manifestation of love between equals. We see love showing itself as mutual tenderness and mutual trustfulness, as consideration, respect, and desire to please, as quick insight into and endeavour to fulfil the wishes of the other, as magnanimity, forbearance. The elements present in the love-emotions of superior to inferior are found here, but mutuality is impressed on all of them. So we may say that the common characteristics of love between equals is desire for mutual help.

Thus we have benevolence, desire for mutual help, and reverence as the three main divisions of the love-emotion, and under these all love emotions may be classified. For all human relations are summed up under the three classes: the relations of superiors to inferiors, of equals to equals, of inferiors to superiors.

She then explains the hate-emotions in the same way:

Hate looking downwards is scorn, and looking upwards is fear. Similarly, hate between equals will show itself in anger, combativeness, disrespect, violence, aggressiveness, jealousy, insolence, etc.—all the emotions which repel man from man when they stand as rivals, face to face, not hand in hand. The common characteristic of hate between equals will thus be mutual injury. And three main characteristics of the hate-emotion are scorn, desire for mutual injury, and fear.

Love is characterised in all its manifestations by sympathy, self-sacrifice, the desire to give; these are its essential factors, whether as benevolence, as desire for mutual help, as reverence. For all these directly serve attraction, bring about union, are of the very nature of love. Hence love is of the spirit; for sympathy is the feeling for another as one would feel for oneself; self-sacrifice is the recognition of the claim of the other, as oneself; giving is the condition of spiritual life. Thus love is seen to belong to spirit, to the life-side of the universe.

Hate, on the other hand, is characterised in all its manifestations by antipathy, self-aggrandisement, the desire to take; these are its essential factors, whether as scorn, desire for mutual injury, or fear. All these directly serve repulsion, driving one apart from another. Hence, hate is of matter, emphasises manifoldness and differences, is essentially separateness, belongs to the form-side of the universe.

CHAPTER III

THE ABSORPTION OF VITALITY

THE GLOBULE

THE vitality globule, though inconceivably minute, is so brilliant that it is often seen even by those who are not in the ordinary sense clairvoyant. Many a man, looking out towards the distant horizon, especially over the sea, will notice against the sky a number of the tiniest possible points of light dashing about in all directions with amazing rapidity. These are the vitality globules, each consisting of seven physical atoms, as shown in Fig. 5c—the Fiery Lives, specks charged with that force which the Hindus call *prāna*. It is often exceedingly difficult to be certain of the exact shade of meaning attached to these Sanskrit terms, because the Indian method of approaching these studies is so different from our own; but I think we may safely take prāna as the equivalent to our vitality.

When this globule is flashing about in the atmosphere, brilliant as it is, it is almost colourless, and shines with a white or slightly golden light. But as soon as it is drawn into the vortex of the force-centre at the spleen it is decomposed and breaks up into streams of different colours, though it does not follow exactly our division of the spectrum. As its component atoms are whirled round the vortex, each of the six spokes seizes upon one of them, so that all the atoms charged with yellow flow along one, and all those charged with green along another, and so on, while the seventh disappears through the centre of the vortex —through the hub of the wheel, as it were. These rays then pass off in different directions, each to do its special work in the vitalization of the body. Plate VIII gives a diagrammatic representation of these paths of the dispersed prāna.

As I have said, the colours of the divisions of prāna are not exactly those which we ordinarily use in the solar spectrum, but rather resemble the arrangement of colours which we see on higher levels in the causal, mental and astral bodies. What we call indigo is divided between the violet ray and the blue ray, so that we find only two divisions there instead of three; but on the other hand what we usually call red is divided into two—rose-red and dark red. The six radiants are therefore violet, blue, green, yellow, orange, and dark red; while the seventh or rose-red atom (more properly the first, since this is the original atom in which the force first appeared) passes down through the centre of the vortex. Vitality is thus clearly sevenfold in its constitution, but it flows through the body in five main streams, as has been stated in some of the Indian books, for after issuing

from the splenic centre the blue and the violet join
into one ray, and so do the orange and the dark red.
(Plate VIII).

THE VIOLET-BLUE RAY

(1) The violet-blue ray flashes upwards to the
throat, where it seems to divide itself, the light blue
remaining to course through and quicken the throat-
centre, while the dark blue and violet pass on into
the brain. The dark blue expends itself in the lower
and central parts of the brain, while the violet floods
the upper part, and appears to give special vigour to
the force-centre at the top of the head, diffusing itself
chiefly through the nine hundred and sixty petals of
the outer part of that centre.

THE YELLOW RAY

(2) The yellow ray is directed to the heart, but
after doing its work there part of it also passes on to
the brain and permeates it, directing itself principally
to the twelve-petalled flower in the midst of the highest
force-centre.

THE GREEN RAY

(3) The green ray floods the abdomen, and while
centring especially in the solar plexus, evidently
vivifies the liver, kidneys and intestines, and the
digestive apparatus generally.

THE ROSE RAY

(4) The rose-coloured ray runs all over the body along the nerves, and is clearly the life of the nervous system. This is the specialized vitality which one man may readily pour into another in whom it is deficient. If the nerves are not fully supplied with this rosy light they become sensitive and intensely irritable, so that the patient finds it almost impossible to remain in one position, and yet gains but little ease when he moves to another. The least noise or touch is agony to him, and he is in a condition of acute misery. The flooding of his nerves with specialized prāna by some healthy person brings instant relief, and a feeling of healing and peace descends upon him. A man in robust health usually absorbs and specializes so much more of this vitality than is actually needed by his own body that he is constantly radiating a torrent of rose-coloured atoms, and so unconsciously pours strength upon his weaker fellows without losing anything himself; or by an effort of his will he can gather together this superfluous energy and aim it intentionally at one whom he wishes to help.

The physical body has a certain blind instinctive consciousness of its own, which we sometimes call the physical elemental. It corresponds in the physical world to the desire-elemental of the astral body; and this consciousness seeks always to protect its body from danger, or to procure for it whatever may be necessary. This is entirely apart from the consciousness of the man himself, and it works equally well during the absence of the ego from the physical body during sleep. All our instinctive movements are due to it, and it is through its activity that the working of the sympathetic system is carried on ceaselessly without any thought or knowledge on our part.

While we are what we call awake, this physical elemental is perpetually occupied in self-defence; he is in a condition of constant vigilance, and he keeps the nerves and muscles always tense. During the night or at any time when we sleep he lets the nerves and muscles relax, and devotes himself specially to the assimilation of vitality and the recuperation of the physical body. He works at this most successfully during the early part of the night, because then there is plenty of vitality, whereas immediately before the dawn the vitality which has been left behind by the sunlight is almost completely exhausted. This is the reason for the feeling of limpness and deadness associated with the small hours of the morning; this is also the reason why sick men so frequently die at that particular time. The same idea is embodied in the old proverb which says that an hour's sleep before midnight is worth two after it. The work of this physical elemental accounts for the strong recuperative influence of sleep, which is often observable even when it is a mere momentary nap.

This vitality is indeed the food of the etheric double, and is just as necessary to it as is material sustenance to the grosser part of the physical body. Hence when the splenic centre is unable for any reason (as through sickness, fatigue or extreme old age) to prepare vitality for the nourishment of the cells of the body, this physical elemental endeavours to draw in for his own use vitality which has already been prepared in the bodies of others; and thus it happens that we often find ourselves weak and exhausted after sitting for a while with a person who is depleted of vitality, because he has drawn the rose-coloured atoms away from us by suction before we were able to extract their energy.

The vegetable kingdom also absorbs this vitality, but seems in most cases to use only a small part of it. Many trees draw from it almost exactly the same constituents as does the higher part of man's etheric body, the result being that when they have used what they require, the atoms which they reject are precisely those charged with the rose-coloured light which is needed for the cells of man's physical body. This is specially the case with such trees as the pine and the eucalyptus; and consequently the very neighbour-hood of these trees gives health and strength to those who are suffering from lack of this part of the vital principle—those whom we call nervous people. They are nervous because the cells of their bodies are hungry, and the nervousness can only be allayed by feeding them; and often the readiest way to do that is thus to supply them from without with the special kind of vitality which they need.

THE ORANGE-RED RAY

(5) The orange-red ray flows to the base of the spine and thence to the generative organs, with which one part of its functions is closely connected. This ray appears to include not only the orange and the darker reds, but also a certain amount of dark purple, as though the spectrum bent round in a circle and the colours began over again at a lower octave.

In the normal man this ray energizes the desires of the flesh, and also seems to enter the blood and help to keep up the heat of the body; but if a man persistently refuses to yield to his lower nature, this ray can by long and determined effort be deflected upwards to the brain, where all three of its constituents undergo a remarkable modification. The orange is raised into pure yellow, and produces a decided intensification of the powers of the intellect; the dark red becomes crimson, and greatly increases the quality of unselfish affection; while the dark purple is transmuted into a lovely pale violet, and quickens the spiritual part of man's nature. The man who achieves this transmutation will find that sensual desires no longer trouble him, and when it becomes necessary for him to arouse the higher layers of the serpent-fire he will be free from the most serious of the dangers of that process. When a man has finally completed this change, this orange-red ray passes straight into the centre at the base of the spine, and from that runs upwards along the hollow of the vertebral column, and so to the brain.

There seems to be a certain correspondence (Table III) between the colours of the streams of prāna flow to the several chakras and the colours assigned by Madame Blavatsky to the principles of man in her diagram in *The Secret Doctrine*, Vol. V, p. 454, Fifth (Adyar) Edition.

Colours of Prānas	Chakras Entered	Colours Given in *S. D.*	Principles Represented
Light blue	Throat	Blue	Ātmā (auric envelope)
Yellow	Heart	Yellow	Buddhi
Dark blue	Brow	Indigo or dark blue	Higher manas
Green	Navel	Green	Kāma manas— lower mind
Rose	Spleen	Red	Kāma rūpa
Violet	Crown	Violet	Etheric double
Orange-red (with another violet)	Root (afterwards crown)	...	...

TABLE III

THE FIVE PRĀNA VĀYUS

In the Hindu books there is frequent reference to the five principal *Vāyus* or prānas. *The Gheranda Samhitā* gives their positions briefly as follows:

The prāna moves always in the heart; the apāna in the sphere of the anus; the samāna in the region of the navel;

the udāna in the throat; and the vyāna pervades the whole body.*

Numerous other books give the same description, and say no more about their functions, but some add a little more information, as follows:

The air called vyāna carries the essential part in all the nerves. Food, as soon as it is eaten, is split into two by that air. Having entered near the anus it separates the solid and liquid portions; having placed the water over the fire, and the solid over the water, the prāna itself, standing under the fire, inflames it slowly. The fire, inflamed by the air, separates substance from the waste. The vyāna air makes the essence go all over, and the waste, forced through the twelve gateways, is ejected from the body. †

The five airs as thus described seem to agree fairly well with the five divisions of vitality which we have observed, as shown in Table IV.

PRĀNA VĀYU AND REGION AFFECTED	RAY OF VITALITY	CHAKRA CHIEFLY AFFECTED
Prāna; heart	Yellow	Cardiac
Apāna; anus	Orange-red	Basic
Samāna; navel	Green	Umbilical
Udāna; throat	Violet-blue	Laryngeal
Vyāna; the entire body	Rose	Splenic

TABLE IV

* Op. cit., vv. 61-2. Sacred Books of the Hindus Series. Trans. Sris Chandra Vidyārnava.

† Garuda Purāna, XV, 40-3. Sacred Books of the Hindus Series. Trans. Wood.

VITALITY AND HEALTH

The flow of vitality in these various currents
regulates the health of the parts of the body with which
they are concerned. If a person is suffering from a
weak digestion, it manifests itself at once to any
person possessing etheric sight, because either the
flow and action of the green stream is sluggish or its
amount is smaller in proportion than it should be.
Where the yellow current is full and strong, it indicates,
or more properly produces, strength and regularity in
the action of the heart. Flowing round that centre,
it also interpenetrates the blood which is driven
through it, and is sent along with it all over the body.
Yet there is enough of it left to extend into the brain
also, and the power of high philosophical and meta-
physical thought appears to depend to a great extent
upon the volume and activity of this yellow stream,
and the corresponding awakening of the twelve-
petalled flower in the middle of the force-centre at
the top of the head.

Thought and emotion of a high spiritual type
seem to depend largely upon the violet ray, whereas
the power of ordinary thought is stimulated by the
action of the blue mingled with part of the yellow.
In some forms of idiocy the flow of vitality to the
brain, both yellow and blue-violet, is almost entirely
inhibited. Unusual activity or volume in the light
blue which is apportioned to the throat-centre is
accompanied by the health and strength of the physical

organs in that part of the body. It gives strength
and elasticity to the vocal cords, so that special brilliance and activity are noticeable in the case of a
public speaker or a great singer. Weakness or disease
in any part of the body is accompanied by a deficiency
in the flow of vitality to that part.

THE FATE OF THE EMPTY ATOMS

As the different streams of atoms do their work,
the charge of vitality is withdrawn from them, precisely
as an electrical charge might be. The atoms bearing
the rose-coloured ray grow gradually paler as they are
swept along the nerves, and are eventually thrown
out from the body through the pores—making thus
what was called in *Man Visible and Invisible* the health-
aura. By the time that they leave the body most of
them have lost the rose-coloured light, so that the
general appearance of the emanation is bluish-white.
That part of the yellow ray which is absorbed into the
blood and carried round with it loses its distinctive
colour in just the same way.

The atoms, when thus emptied of their charge of
vitality, either enter into some of the combinations
which are constantly being made in the body, or pass
out of it through the pores, or through the ordinary
channels. The emptied atoms of the green ray, which
is connected chiefly with digestive processes, seem to
form part of the ordinary waste material of the body,
and to pass out along with it, and that is also the fate

of the atoms of the red-orange ray in the case of the
ordinary man.   The atoms belonging to the blue rays,
which are used in connection with the throat-centre,
generally leave the body in the exhalations of the
breath; and those which compose the dark blue and
violet rays usually pass out from the centre at the
top of the head.

When the student has learnt to deflect the orange-
red rays so that they also move up through the spine,
the empty atoms of both these and the violet-blue
rays pour out from the top of the head in a fiery
cascade which, as we have already seen in Fig. 2, is
frequently imaged as a flame in ancient statues of the
Lord Buddha and other great saints.   These atoms
are thus used again as physical vehicles for some of
the glorious and beneficent forces which highly-
evolved men radiate from that crown chakra.

When empty of the vital force the atoms are once
more precisely like any other atoms, except that they
have evolved somewhat through the use that has been
made of them.   The body absorbs such of them as
it needs, so that they form part of the various combinations which are constantly being made, while others
which are not required for such purposes are cast
out through any channel that happens to be convenient.

The flow of vitality into or through any centre,
or even its intensification, must not be confused with
the entirely different development of the centre which
is brought about by the awakening of the higher
levels of the serpent-fire at a later stage in man's

evolution, with which we shall deal in the next chapter. We all draw in vitality and specialize it, but many of us do not utilize it to the full, because in various ways our lives are not as pure and healthy and reasonable as they should be. One who coarsens his body by the use of meat, alcohol or tobacco can never employ his vitality to the full in the same way as can a man of purer living. A particular individual of impure life may be, and often is, stronger in the physical body than certain other men who are purer; that is a matter of their respective karma; but other things being equal, the man of pure life has an immense advantage.

All the colours of this order of vitality are etheric, yet it will be seen that their action presents certain correspondences with the signification attached to similar hues in the astral body. Clearly, right thought and right feeling react upon the physical body and increase its power to assimilate the vitality which is necessary for its well-being. It is reported that the Lord Buddha once said that the first step on the road to Nirvāna is perfect physical health; and assuredly the way to attain that is to follow the Noble Eightfold Path which he has indicated. " Seek ye first the Kingdom of God and his righteousness, and all these things shall be added unto you "—yes, even physical health as well.

VITALITY AND MAGNETISM

The vitality coursing along the nerves must not be confused with what we usually call the magnetism of the man—his own nerve-fluid, specialized within the spine, and composed of the primary life-force intermingled with the kundalinī. It is this fluid which keeps up the constant circulation of etheric matter along the nerves, corresponding to the circulation of blood through the arteries and veins; and as oxygen is conveyed by the blood to all parts of the body, so vitality is conveyed along the nerves by this etheric current. The particles of the etheric part of man's body are constantly changing, just as are those of the denser part; along with the food which we eat and the air which we breathe we take in etheric matter, and this is assimilated by the etheric part of the body. Etheric matter is constantly being thrown off from the pores, just as is gaseous matter, so that when two persons are close together each necessarily absorbs much of the physical emanations of the other.

When one person mesmerizes another, the operator by an effort of will gathers together a great deal of this magnetism and throws it into the subject, pushing back his victim's nerve-fluid, and filling its place with his own. As the brain is the centre of this nervous circulation, this brings that part of the subject's body which is affected under the control of the manipulator's brain instead of the victim's and so the latter feels what the mesmerist wishes him to feel. If the recipient's brain be emptied of his own magnetism and filled with that of the performer, the former can think and act only as the latter wills that he should think and act; he is for the time entirely dominated.

Even when the magnetizer is trying to cure, and is pouring strength into the man, he inevitably gives along with the vitality much of his own emanations. It is obvious that any disease which the mesmerizer happens to have may readily be conveyed to the subject in this way; and another even more important consideration is that, though his health may be perfect from the medical point of view, there are mental and moral diseases as well as physical, and that, as astral and mental matter are thrown into the subject by the mesmerist along with the physical current, these also are frequently transferred.

Nevertheless, a man who is pure in thought and filled with the earnest desire to help his fellows may often do much by mesmerism to relieve suffering, if he will take the trouble to study this subject of the currents which enter the body through the chakras and flow along the nerves. What is it that the mesmerist pours into his subject? It may be either the nerve-ether or the vitality, or both. Supposing a patient to be seriously weakened or exhausted, so that he has lost the power to specialize the life-fluid for himself, the mesmerist may renew his stock by pouring some of his own upon the quivering nerves, and so produce a rapid recovery. The process is analogous to what is often done in the case of food. When a person reaches a certain stage of weakness the stomach loses the power to digest, and so the body is not properly nourished, and the feebleness is thereby increased. The remedy adopted in that case is to present to the stomach food already partially digested by means of pepsin or other similar preparations; this can probably be assimilated, and thus strength is gained. Just so, a man who is unable to specialize for himself may still absorb what has been already prepared by another, and so gain strength to make an effort to resume the normal action of the etheric organs. In many cases of debility that is all that is needed.

There are other instances in which congestion of some kind has taken place, the vital fluid has not circulated properly, and the nerve-aura is sluggish and unhealthy. Then the obvious course of proceeding is to replace it by healthy nerve-ether from without; but there are several ways in which this may be done. Some magnetizers simply employ brute force, and steadily pour in resistless floods of their own ether in the hope of washing away that which needs removal. Success may be attained along these lines, though with the expenditure of a good deal more energy than is necessary. A more scientific method is that which goes to work somewhat more quietly, and first withdraws the congested or diseased matter, and then replaces it by healthier nerve-ether, thus gradually stimulating the sluggish current into activity. If the patient has a headache, for example, there will almost certainly be a congestion of noxious ether about some part of his brain, and the first step is to draw that away.

How is this to be managed? Just in the same way as the out-pouring of strength is managed—by an exercise of the will. We must not forget that these finer subdivisions of matter are readily moulded or affected by the action of the human will. The mesmerist may make passes, but they are at the most nothing but the pointing of his gun in a certain direction, while his will is the powder that moves the ball and produces the result, the fluid being the shot sent out. A mesmerizer who understands his business can manage as well without passes if he wishes; I have known one who never employed them, but simply looked at his subject. The only use of the hand is to concentrate the fluid, and perhaps to help the imagination of the operator; for to will strongly he must believe firmly, and the action no doubt makes it easier for him to realize what he is doing.

Just as a man may pour out magnetism by an effort of will, so may he draw it away by an effort of will; and in this case also he may often use a gesture of the hands to help him. In dealing with the headache, he would probably lay his hands upon the forehead of the patient, and think of them as sponges steadily drawing out the deleterious magnetism from the brain. That he is actually producing the result of which he thinks, he will be very likely soon to discover, for unless he takes precautions to cast off the bad magnetism which he is absorbing, he will either himself feel the headache or begin to suffer from a pain in the arm and hand with which the operation is being performed. He is actually drawing into himself diseased matter, and it is necessary for his comfort and well-being that he should dispose of it before it obtains a permanent lodgment in his body.

He should therefore adopt some definite plan to get rid of it, and the simplest is just to throw it away, to shake it from the hands as one would shake water. Although he does not see it, the matter which he has withdrawn is physical, and we can deal with it by physical means. It is therefore necessary that he should not neglect these precautions, and that he should not forget to wash his hands carefully after curing a headache or any malady of that nature. Then, after he has removed the cause of the evil, he proceeds to pour in good strong healthy magnetism to take its place, and to protect the patient against the return of the disease. One can see that in the case of any nervous affection this method would have manifold advantages. In most of such cases what is wrong is an irregularity of the fluids which course along the nerves; either they are congested, or they are sluggish in their flow, or on the other hand they may be too rapid; they may be deficient in quantity, or poor in quality. If we administer drugs of any sort, at the best we can act only upon the physical nerve, and through it to some limited extent upon the fluids surrounding it; whereas mesmerism acts directly upon the fluids themselves, and so goes straight to the root of the evil.

CHAPTER IV

THE DEVELOPMENT OF THE CHAKRAS

THE FUNCTIONS OF THE AWAKENED CENTRES

BESIDES keeping alive the physical vehicle, the force-centres have another function, which comes into play only when they are awakened into full activity. Each of the etheric centres corresponds to an astral centre, though as the astral centre is a vortex in four dimensions it has an extension in a direction quite different from the etheric, and consequently is by no means always co-terminous with it, though some part is always coincident. The etheric vortex is always on the surface of the etheric body, but the astral centre is frequently quite in the interior of that vehicle.

The function of each of the etheric centres when fully aroused is to bring down into physical consciousness whatever may be the quality inherent in the astral centre which corresponds to it; so, before cataloguing the results to be obtained by arousing the etheric centres into activity, it may be well to consider what is done by each of the astral centres, although these latter are already in full activity in all cultured people

of later races. What effect, then, has the quickening
of each of these astral centres produced in the astral
body?

The Astral Centres

The first of these centres, as has already been
explained, is the home of the serpent-fire. This force
exists on all planes, and by its activity the rest of the
centres are aroused. We must think of the astral
body as having been originally an almost inert mass,
with nothing but the vaguest consciousness, with no
definite power of doing anything, and no clear knowledge of the world which surrounded it. The first
thing that happened, then, was the awakening of that
force in the man at the astral level. When awakened
it moved on to the second centre, corresponding to
the physical spleen, and through it vitalized the whole
astral body, enabling the person to travel consciously,
though with only a vague conception as yet of what
he encountered on his journeys.

Then it moved on to the third, that corresponding
to the navel, and vivified it, thereby awakening in the
astral body the power of feeling—a sensitiveness to
all sorts of influences, though without as yet anything
like the definite comprehension that comes from seeing
or hearing.

The fourth centre, when awakened, endowed the
man with the power to comprehend and sympathize
with the vibrations of other astral entities, so that he

could instinctively understand something of their feelings.

The awakening of the fifth, that corresponding to the throat, gave him the power of hearing on the astral plane; that is to say, it caused the development of that sense which in the astral world produces on our consciousness the effect which on the physical plane we call hearing.

The development of the sixth, that corresponding to the centre between the eyebrows, in a similar manner produced astral sight—the power to perceive definitely the shape and nature of astral objects, instead of vaguely sensing their presence.

The arousing of the seventh, that corresponding to the top of the head, rounded off and completed for him the astral life, and endowed him with the perfection of its faculties.

With regard to this centre a certain difference seems to exist, according to the type to which men belong. For many of us the astral vortices corresponding to the sixth and seventh of these centres both converge upon the pituitary body, and for those people the pituitary body (Fig. 8) is practically the only direct link between the physical and the higher planes. Another type of people, however, while still attaching the sixth centre to the pituitary body, bend or slant the seventh until its vortex coincides with the atrophied organ called the pineal gland (Fig. 8), which is by people of that type vivified and made into a line of communication directly with the lower mental, without

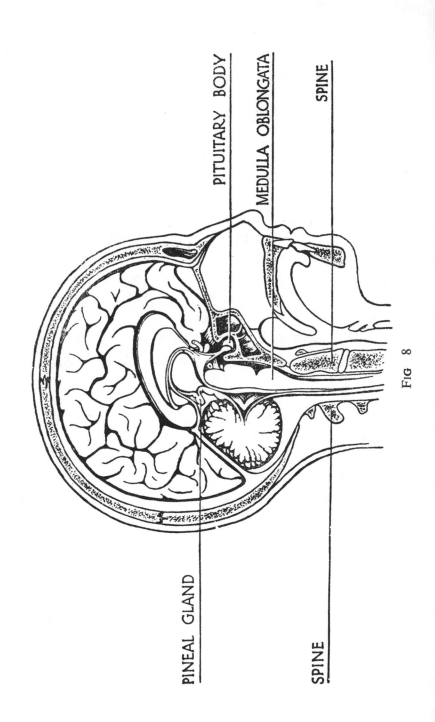

PINEAL GLAND

SPINE

PITUITARY BODY

MEDULLA OBLONGATA

SPINE

Fig 8

apparently passing through the intermediate astral plane in the ordinary way. It was for this type that Madame Blavatsky was writing when she laid such emphasis upon the awakening of that organ. Dr. Besant also mentions this fact that the starting-point of development begins at different levels with different persons, in the following passage from *A Study in Consciousness*:

> The building of the centres and the gradual organization of them into wheels, can be begun from any vehicle, and will be begun in any individual from that vehicle which represents the special type of temperament to which he belongs. According as a man belongs to one typical temperament or another, so will be the place of the greatest activity in the building up of all the vehicles, in the gradual making of them into effective instruments of consciousness to be expressed on the physical plane. This centre of activity may be in the physical, astral, lower, or higher mental body. In any of these, or even higher still, according to the temperamental type, this centre will be found in the principle which marks out the temperamental type, and from that it works "upwards" or "downwards", shaping the vehicles so as to make them suitable for the expression of that temperament.[1]

ASTRAL SENSES

Thus these centres to some extent take the place of sense-organs for the astral body; yet without proper qualification that expression would be decidedly misleading, for it must never be forgotten that though, in order to make ourselves intelligible, we constantly have to speak of astral seeing or astral hearing, all that we really mean by those expressions is the faculty of responding to such vibrations as convey to the man's

[1] *Op. cit.*, p. 252.

consciousness, when he is functioning in his astral body, information of the same character as that conveyed to him by his eyes and ears while he is in the physical body.

But in the entirely different astral conditions specialized organs are not necessary for the attainment of this result. There is matter in every part of the astral body which is capable of such response, and consequently the man functioning in that vehicle sees equally well the objects behind him, above him, and beneath him, without needing to turn his head. The centres, therefore, cannot be described as organs in the ordinary sense of the word, since it is not through them that the man sees or hears, as he does here through the eyes and ears. Yet it is upon their vivification that the power of exercising these astral senses depends, each of them as it is developed giving to the whole astral body the power of response to a new set of vibrations.

As all the particles of the astral body are constantly flowing and swirling about like those of boiling water, all of them in turn pass through each of the centres or vortices, so that each centre in its turn evokes in all the particles of the body the power of receptivity to a certain set of vibrations, and so all the astral senses are equally active in all parts of the body. But even when these astral senses are fully awakened it by no means follows that the man will be able to bring through into his physical body any consciousness of their action.

THE AROUSING OF KUNDALINĪ

While all this astral awakening was taking place, then, the man in his physical consciousness knew nothing whatever of it. The only way in which the dense body can be brought to share all these advantages is by repeating that process of awakening with the etheric centres. That may be achieved in various ways, according to the school of yoga which the student is practising.

Seven schools of yoga are recognized in India: 1. Rāja Yoga; 2. Karma Yoga; 3. Jnāna Yoga; 4. Hatha Yoga; 5. Laya Yoga; 6. Bhakti Yoga; 7. Mantra Yoga. I have given some account of them in the second edition of *The Masters and the Path*, and Professor Wood has described them fully in his book *Rāja Yoga; the Occult Training of the Hindus*. They all recognize the existence and the importance of the chakras, and each has its own method of developing them. The plan of the Rāja Yogi is to meditate upon each in turn and bring them into activity by sheer force of will—a scheme which has much to recommend it. The school which pays most attention to them is that of Laya Yoga, and its system is to arouse the higher potentialities of the serpent-fire, and force it through the centres one by one.

That arousing needs a determined and a long continued effort of the will, for to bring that first chakra into full activity is precisely to awaken the inner layers of the serpent-fire. When once that is aroused, it is by its tremendous force that the other centres are vivified. Its effect on the other etheric wheels is to bring into the physical consciousness the powers which were aroused by the development of their corresponding astral chakras.

The Awakening of the Etheric Chakras

When the second of the etheric centres, that at the spleen, is awakened, the man is enabled to remember his vague astral journeys, though sometimes only very partially. The effect of a slight and accidental stimulation of this centre is often to produce half-remembrance of a blissful sensation of flying through the air.

When the third centre, that at the navel, comes into activity, the man begins in the physical body to be conscious of all kinds of astral influences, vaguely feeling that some of them are friendly and others hostile, or that some places are pleasant and others unpleasant, without in the least knowing why.

Stimulation of the fourth, that at the heart, makes the man instinctively aware of the joys and sorrows of others, and sometimes even causes him to reproduce in himself by sympathy their physical aches and pains.

The arousing of the fifth, that at the throat, enables him to hear voices, which sometimes make all kinds of suggestions to him. Also sometimes he hears music, or other less pleasant sounds. When it is fully working it makes the man clairaudient as far as the etheric and astral planes are concerned.

When the sixth, between the eyebrows, becomes vivified, the man begins to see things, to have various sorts of waking visions, sometimes of places, sometimes of people. In its earlier development, when it is only just beginning to be awakened, it often means nothing more than half-seeing landscapes and clouds of colour. The full arousing of this brings about clairvoyance.

The centre between the eyebrows is connected with sight in yet another way. It is through it that the power of magnification of minute physical objects is exercised. A tiny flexible tube of etheric matter is projected from the centre of it, resembling a microscopic snake with something like an eye at the end of it. This is the special organ used in that form of clairvoyance, and the eye at the end of it can be expanded or contracted, the effect being to change the power of magnification according to the size of the object which is being examined. This is what is meant in ancient books when mention is made of the capacity to make oneself large or small at will. To examine an atom one develops an organ of vision commensurate in size with the atom. This little snake projecting from the centre of the forehead was symbolized upon the head-dress of the Pharaoh of Egypt, who as the chief priest of his country was supposed to possess this among many other occult powers.

When the seventh centre is quickened, the man is able by passing through it to leave his body in full consciousness, and also to return to it without the usual break, so that his consciousness will be continuous through night and day. When the fire has been passed through all these centres in a certain order (which varies for different types of people) the consciousness becomes continuous up to the entry into the heaven-world at the end of the life on the astral plane, no difference being made by either the temporary separation from the physical body during sleep or the permanent division at death.

CASUAL CLAIRVOYANCE

Before this is done, however, the man may have many glimpses of the astral world, for specially strong vibrations may at any time galvanize one or other of the chakras into temporary activity, without arousing the serpent-fire at all; or it may happen that the fire may be partially roused, and in this way also spasmodic clairvoyance may be produced for the time. For this fire exists, as we have said, in seven layers or seven degrees of force, and it often happens that a man who exerts his will in the effort to arouse it may succeed in affecting one layer only, and so when he thinks that he has done the work he may find it ineffective, and may have to do it all over again many times, digging gradually deeper and deeper, until not only the surface is stirred but the very heart of the fire is in full activity.

THE DANGER OF PREMATURE AWAKENING

This fiery power, as it is called in *The Voice of the Silence*, is in very truth like liquid fire as it rushes through the body when it has been aroused by the will; and the course through which it ought to move is spiral like the coils of a serpent. In its awakened state it may be called the World's Mother in another sense than that already mentioned, because through it our various vehicles may be vivified, so that the higher worlds may open before us in succession.

For the ordinary person it lies at the base of the spine unawakened, and its very presence unsuspected, during the whole of his life; and it is indeed far better to allow it thus to remain dormant until the man has made definite moral development, until his will is strong enough to control it and his thoughts pure enough to enable him to face its awakening without injury. No one should experiment with it without definite instruction from a teacher who thoroughly understands the subject, for the dangers connected with it are very real and terribly serious. Some of them are purely physical. Its uncontrolled movement often produces intense physical pain, and it may readily tear tissues and even destroy physical life. This, however, is the least of the evils of which it is capable, for it may do permanent injury to vehicles higher than the physical.

One very common effect of rousing it prematurely is that it rushes downwards in the body instead of upwards, and thus excites the most undesirable passions—excites them and intensifies their effects to such a degree that it becomes impossible for the man to resist them, because a force has been brought into play in whose presence he is as helpless as a swimmer before the jaws of a shark. Such men become satyrs, monsters of depravity, because they are in the grasp of a force which is out of all proportion to the ordinary human power of resistance. They may probably gain certain supernormal powers, but these will be such as will bring them into touch with a lower order of evolution with which humanity is intended to hold no commerce, and to escape from its awful thraldom may take them more than one incarnation.

I am not in any way exaggerating the horror of this thing, as a person to whom it was all a matter of hearsay might unwittingly do. I have myself been consulted by people upon whom this awful fate has already come, and I have seen with my own eyes what happened to them. There is a school of black magic which purposely utilizes this power for such purposes, in order that through it may be vivified a certain lower force-centre which is never used in that way by the followers of the Good Law. Some writers deny the existence of such a centre; but Brāhmanas of Southern India assure me that there are certain yogis who teach their pupils to use it—though of course not necessarily with evil intent. Still, the risk is too great to be worth taking when one can achieve the same results in a safer way.

Even apart from this greatest of its dangers, the premature unfoldment of the higher aspects of kundalinī has many other unpleasant possibilities. It intensifies everything in the man's nature, and it reaches the lower and evil qualities more readily than the good. In the mental body, for example, ambition is very quickly aroused, and soon swells to an incredibly inordinate degree. It would be likely to bring with it a great intensification of the power of intellect, but at the same time it would produce abnormal and satanic pride, such as is quite inconceivable to the ordinary man. It is not wise for a man to think that he is prepared to cope with any force that may arise within his body; this is no ordinary energy, but something resistless. Assuredly no uninstructed man should ever try to awaken it, and if such an one finds that it has been aroused by accident he should at once consult some one who fully understands these matters.

I am specially refraining from any explanation as to how this arousing is to be done, nor do I mention the order in which the force (when aroused) should be passed through these various centres, *for that should by no means be attempted except at the express suggestion of a Master, who will watch over His pupils during the various stages of the experiment.*

I should like most solemnly to warn all students against making any effort whatever in the direction of awakening these tremendous forces, except under such qualified tuition, for I have myself seen many cases of the terrible effects which follow from ignorant and ill-advised meddling with these very serious matters. The force is a tremendous reality, one of the great basic facts of nature, and most emphatically it is not a thing with which to play, not a matter to be lightly taken in hand, for to experiment with it without understanding it is far more dangerous than it would be for a child to play with nitroglycerine. As is very truly said in *The Hathayoga Pradīpikā*: " It gives liberation to yogis and bondage to fools." (III, 107.)

In matters such as these, students so often seem to think that some special exception to the laws of nature will be made in their case, that some special intervention of providence will save them from the consequences of their folly. Assuredly nothing of that sort will happen, and the man who wantonly provokes an explosion is quite likely to become its first victim. It would save much trouble and disappointment if students could be induced to understand that in all matters connected with occultism we mean just exactly and literally what we say, and that it is applicable in every case without exception. For there is no such thing as favouritism in the working of the great laws of the universe.

Everybody wants to try all possible experiments; everybody is convinced that he is quite ready for the highest possible teaching and for any sort of development, and no one is willing to work patiently along at the improvement of character, and to devote his time and his energies to doing something useful for the work of The Society, waiting for all these other

things until a Master shall announce that he is ready
for them. As I have already said in the previous
chapter in another connection, the old aphorism still
remains true: " Seek ye first the Kingdom of God
and His righteousness, and all these things shall be
added unto you."

THE SPONTANEOUS AWAKENING OF KUNDALINĪ

There are some cases in which the inner layers
of this fire awaken spontaneously, so that a dull glow
is felt; it may even begin to move of itself, though
this is rare. When this happens, it may cause great
pain, as, since the passages are not prepared for it,
it would have to clear its way by actually burning up
a great deal of etheric dross—a process that cannot
but engender suffering. When it thus awakes of itself
or is accidentally aroused, it usually tries to pass up
the interior of the spine, following the course already
taken by its lowest and gentlest manifestation. If it
be possible, the will should be set in motion to arrest
its upward movement, but if that proves to be impossible (as is most likely) no alarm need be felt. It
will probably flash out through the head and escape
into the surrounding atmosphere, and it is likely
that no harm will result beyond a slight weakening.
Nothing worse than a temporary loss of consciousness
need be apprehended. The really appalling dangers
are connected not with its upward rush, but with the
possibility of its turning downwards and inwards.

Its principal function in connection with occult development is that, by being sent through the force-centres in the etheric body, as above described, it quickens these chakras and makes them more fully available as gates of connection between the physical and astral bodies. It is said in *The Voice of the Silence* that when the serpent-fire reaches the centre between the eyebrows and fully vivifies it, it confers the power of hearing the voice of the Master—which means in this case the voice of the ego or higher self. The reason for this statement is that when the pituitary body is brought into working order it forms a perfect link with the astral vehicle, so that through it all communications from within can be received.

It is not only this chakra; all the higher force-centres have presently to be awakened, and each must be made responsive to all kinds of influences from the various astral subplanes. This development will come to all in due course, but most people cannot gain it during the present incarnation, if it is the first in which they have begun to take these matters seriously in hand. Some Indians might succeed in doing so, as their bodies are by heredity more adaptable than most others; but it is really for the majority the work of a later Round altogether. The conquest of the serpent-fire has to be repeated in each incarnation, since the vehicles are new each time, but after it has been once thoroughly achieved these repetitions will be an easy matter. It must be remembered that its action varies with different types of people; some, for example, would see the higher self rather than hear its voice. Again, this connection with the higher has many stages; for the personality it means the influence of the ego, but for the ego himself it means the power of the Monad, and for the Monad in turn it means to become a conscious expression of the Logos.

PERSONAL EXPERIENCE

It may be of use if I mention my own experience in this matter. In the earlier part of my residence in India forty-two years ago I made no effort to rouse the fire—not indeed knowing very much about it, and having the opinion that, in order to do anything with it, it was necessary to be born with a specially psychic body, which I did not possess. But one day one of the Masters made a suggestion to me with regard to a certain kind of meditation which would evoke this force. Naturally I at once put the suggestion into practice, and in course of time was successful. I have no doubt, however, that He watched the experiment, and would have checked me if it had become dangerous. I am told that there are Indian ascetics who teach this to their pupils, of course keeping them under careful supervision during the process. But I do not myself know of any such, nor should I have confidence in them unless they were specially recommended by some one whom I knew to be possessed of real knowledge.

People often ask me what I advise them to do with regard to the arousing of this force. I advise them to do exactly what I myself did. I recommend them to throw themselves into Theosophical work and wait until they receive a definite command from some Master who will undertake to superintend their psychic development, continuing in the meantime all the ordinary exercises of meditation that are known to them. They should not care in the least whether such development comes in this incarnation or in the next, but should regard the matter from the point of view of the ego and not of the personality, feeling absolutely certain that the Masters are always watching for those whom They can help, that it is entirely impossible for anyone to be overlooked, and that They will unquestionably give Their directions when They think that the right time has come.

I have never heard that there is any sort of age limit with regard to the development, and I do not see that age should make any difference, so long as one has perfect health; but the health is a necessity, for only a strong body can endure the strain, which is much more serious than anyone who has not made the attempt can possibly imagine.

The force when aroused must be very strictly controlled, and it must be moved through the centres in an order which differs for people of different types. The movement also, to be effective, must be made in a particular way, which the Master will explain when the time comes.

THE ETHERIC WEB

I have said that the astral and etheric centres are in very close correspondence; but between them, and interpenetrating them in a manner not readily describable, is a sheath or web of closely woven texture, a sheath composed of a single layer of physical atoms much compressed and permeated by a special form of vital force. The divine life which normally descends from the astral body to the physical is so attuned as to pass through this with perfect ease, but it is an absolute barrier to all other forces—all which cannot use the atomic matter of both the planes. This web is the protection provided by nature to prevent a premature opening up of communication between the planes—a development which could lead to nothing but injury.

It is this which under normal conditions prevents clear recollection of what has happened during sleep, and it is this also which causes the momentary unconsciousness which always occurs at death. But for this merciful provision the ordinary man, who knows nothing about all these things and is entirely unprepared to meet them, could at any moment be brought by any astral entity under the influence of forces to cope with which would be entirely beyond his strength. He would be liable to constant obsession by any being on the astral plane who desired to seize upon his vehicles.

It will therefore be readily understood that any injury to this web is a serious disaster. There are several ways in which injury may come, and it behoves us to use our best endeavours to guard against it. It may come either by accident or by continued malpractice. Any great shock to the astral body, such for example as a sudden terrible fright, may rend apart this delicate organism and, as it is commonly expressed, drive the man mad. (Of course there are other ways in which fear may cause insanity, but this is one.) A tremendous outburst of anger may also produce the same effect. Indeed it may follow upon any exceedingly strong emotion of an evil character which produces a kind of explosion in the astral body.

THE EFFECTS OF ALCOHOL AND DRUGS

The malpractices which may more gradually injure this protective web are of two classes—use of alcohol or narcotic drugs, and the deliberate endeavour to throw open the doors which nature has kept closed, by means of such a process as is described in spiritualistic parlance as sitting for development. Certain drugs and drinks—notably alcohol and all the narcotics, including tobacco—contain matter which on breaking up volatilizes, and some of it passes from the physical plane to the astral. (Even tea and coffee contain this matter, but in quantities so infinitesimal that it is usually only after long-continued abuse of them that the effect manifests itself.)

When this takes place in the body of man these constituents rush out through the chakras in the opposite direction to that for which they are intended, and in doing this repeatedly they seriously injure and finally destroy the delicate web. This deterioration or destruction may be brought about in two different ways, according to the type of the person concerned and to the proportion of the constituents in his etheric and astral bodies. First, the rush of volatilizing matter actually burns away the web, and therefore leaves the door open to all sorts of irregular forces and evil influences.

The second result is that these volatile constituents, in flowing through, somehow harden the atom, so that its pulsation is to a large extent checked and crippled, and it is no longer capable of being vitalized by the particular type of force which welds it into a web. The result of this is a kind of ossification of the web, so that instead of having too much coming through from one plane to the other, we have very little of any kind coming through.

We may see the effects of both these types of deterioration in the case of men who yield themselves to drunkenness. Some of those who are affected in the former way fall into delirium tremens, obsession or insanity; but those are after all comparatively rare. Far more common is the second type of deterioration— the case in which we have a kind of general deadening down of the man's qualities, resulting in gross materialism, brutality and animalism, in the loss of all finer feelings and of the power to control himself. He no longer feels any sense of responsibility; he may love

his wife and children when sober, but when the fit of
drunkenness comes upon him he will use the money
which should have brought bread for them to satisfy
his own bestial cravings, the affection and the responsibility having apparently entirely disappeared.

THE EFFECT OF TOBACCO

The second type of effect is very commonly to be
seen among those who are slaves of the tobacco habit.
Its effects are obvious in the physical, astral and
mental bodies.

It permeates the man physically with exceedingly
impure particles, causing emanations so grossly
material that they are frequently perceptible to the
sense of smell.   Astrally it not only introduces impurity
but it also tends to deaden many of the vibrations,
and it is for this reason that it is found to " soothe
the nerves ", as it is called.   But of course for occult
progress we do not want the vibrations deadened,
nor the astral body weighed down with poisonous
particles.   We need the capacity of answering instantly
to all possible wave-lengths, and yet at the same time
we must have perfect control, so that our desires
shall be as horses guided by the intelligent mind to
draw us where we will, not to run away with us wildly,
as does the tobacco habit, and carry us into situations
where our higher nature knows that it ought never
to be found.   Its results after death are also of the
most distressing character; it causes a sort of ossification

and paralysis of the astral body, so that for a long time (extending to weeks and months) the man remains helpless, supine, scarcely conscious, shut up as though in a prison, unable to communicate with his friends, dead for the time to all higher influences. Is it worth while incurring all these penalties for the sake of a petty indulgence? For any person who really means to develop his vehicles, to awaken his chakras, to make progress along the path of holiness, tobacco is undoubtedly to be sedulously avoided.

All impressions which pass from one plane to the other are intended to come only through the atomic subplanes, as I have said; but when this deadening process sets in, it presently infects not only other atomic matter, but matter of even the second and third subplanes, so that the only communication between the astral and the etheric is when some force acting on the lower subplanes (upon which only unpleasant and evil influences are to be found) happens to be strong enough to compel a response by the violence of its vibration.

THE OPENING OF THE DOORS

Nevertheless, though nature takes such precautions to guard these centres, she by no means intends that they shall always be kept rigidly closed. There is a proper way in which they may be opened. Perhaps it would be more correct to say that the intention is not that the doors should be opened any wider than their present position, but that the man should so develop himself that he can bring a great deal more through the recognized channel.

The consciousness of the ordinary man cannot yet use pure atomic matter either in the physical body or in the astral, and therefore there is normally no possibility for him of conscious communication at will between the two planes. The proper way to obtain that is to purify both the vehicles until the atomic matter in both is fully vitalized, so that all communications between the two may be able to pass by that road. In that case the web retains to the fullest degree its position and activity, and yet is no longer a barrier to the perfect communication, while it still continues to fulfil its purpose of preventing the close contact between lower subplanes which would permit all sorts of undesirable influences to pass through.

That is why we are always adjured to wait for the unfolding of psychic powers until they come in the natural course of events as a consequence of the development of character, as we see from the study of these force-centres that they surely will. That is the natural evolution; that is the only really safe way, for by it the student obtains all the benefits and avoids all the dangers. That is the Path which our Masters have trodden in the past; that therefore is the Path for us today.

CHAPTER V

THE LAYA YOGA

THE HINDU BOOKS

IT is nearly twenty years since I wrote the major part of the information about the chakras which appears in the preceding pages, and I had at that time but a very slight acquaintance with the extensive literature which exists on the subject in the Sanskrit language. Since then, however, several important works on the chakras have become available in English, among which are *The Serpent Power* (which is a translation by Arthur Avalon of *The Shatchakra Nirupana*), *Thirty Minor Upanishads*, translated by K. Nārāyanaswami Aiyar, and *The Shiva Samhitā*, translated by Sris Chandra Vidyārnava. These works deal extensively with the special subject of chakras, but there are many others which touch upon the centres in a more casual way. Avalon's book gives us an excellent series of coloured illustrations of all the chakras, in the symbolical form in which they are always drawn by the Hindu yogis. This department of Hindu science is gradually becoming known in the West; for the benefit of my readers I will attempt to give a very brief outline of it here.

THE INDIAN LIST OF CHAKRAS

The chakras mentioned in these Sanskrit books are the same as those which we see today, except that as I have already said, they always substitute their Svādhishthāna centre for that at the spleen. They differ slightly among themselves as to the number of petals, but on the whole they agree with us, though for some reason they do not include the centre at the top of head, confining themselves to six chakras only, and calling the crown centre the Shasrāra Padma—the lotus of a thousand petals. The smaller chakra of twelve petals within this crown centre was observed by them, and is duly noted. They speak of two petals instead of ninety-six in the sixth chakra, but they refer no doubt to the two divisions of the disc of that centre, mentioned in Chapter I.

The discrepancies as to the number of petals are not important; for example, *The Yoga Kundalinī Upanishad* speaks of sixteen petals in the heart chakra instead of twelve, and *The Dhyānabindu Upanishad* and *The Shāndilya Upanishad* both mention twelve spokes instead of ten in the navel chakra. A number of works also refer to another chakra that is below the heart, and to several centres between the brow chakra and the crown lotus, all as being of great importance. *The Dhyānabindu Upanishad* says that the lotus of the heart has eight petals, but its description of the use of that chakra in meditation indicates (as we shall see later) that it is probably referring to the secondary heart chakra to which I have just referred. In the matter of the colours of the petals there are also some disagreements, as will be seen from Table V, comparing some of the principal works with our own list.

COLOURS OF LOTUS PETALS				
CHAKRA	OUR OBSERVATIONS	SHATCHAKRA NIRŪPANA	SHIVA SAMHITĀ	GARUDA PURĀNA
1	Fiery orange-red	Red	Red	...
2	Glowing, sunlike	Vermilion	Vermilion	Sunlike
3	Various reds and greens	Blue	Golden	Red
4	Golden	Vermilion	Deep red	Golden
5	Blue, silvery, gleaming	Smoky purple	Brilliant gold	Moonlike
6	Yellow and purple	White	White	Red

TABLE V

It is not surprising that such differences as these should be on record, for there are unquestionably variants in the chakras of different people and races, as well as in the faculties of observers. What we have recorded in Chapter I is the result of careful observation on the part of a number of Western students, who have taken every precaution to compare notes and to verify what they have seen.

7

The drawings of the chakras made by the Hindu yogis for the use of their pupils are always symbolical, and bear no relation to the actual appearance of the chakra, except that an attempt is usually made to indicate the colour and the number of petals. In the centre of each such drawing we shall find a geometrical form, a letter of the Sanskrit alphabet, an animal, and two deities, one male and the other female. We give in Fig. 9 a reproduction of the drawing of the heart chakra, borrowed from Arthur Avalon's *The Serpent Power*. We shall endeavour to explain what is understood by the various symbols.

THE FIGURES OF THE CHAKRAS

The object of Laya or Kundalinī Yoga is the same as that of every other form of Indian yoga, to unite the soul with God; and for this purpose it is always necessary to make three kinds of efforts—those of love, of thought and of action. Though in a particular school of yoga the will must be especially used (as is the case in the teaching of *The Yoga Sutras*), and in another great love is chiefly prescribed (as in the instruction given by Shrī Krishna to Arjuna in *The Bhagavad Gītā*), still it is always proclaimed that attainments must be made in all three directions. Thus Patanjali propounds for the candidate at the beginning a course of *tapas* or purificatory effort, *svādhyāya* or study of spiritual things, and *Īshvara pranidhāna*, or devotion to God at all times. Shrī

Krishna, similarly, after explaining to His pupil that wisdom is the most valuable instrument of service, the greatest offering that one can make, adds that it may be learnt only by devotion, enquiry and service,

FIG. 9

concluding His statement with the significant words:
" The Wise Ones, Seers of the Truth, will teach you
the wisdom." In *At the Feet of the Master*, which
is the most modern rendering of the Eastern teaching,
the same triplicity appears, for the qualifications
include discrimination, the practice of good conduct,
and the development of love towards God, Guru or
Teacher, and man.

To understand these diagrams of the chakras
which are used by Indian yogis, it must be borne in
mind that they are intended to assist the aspirant in
all these three lines of progress. It is necessary that he
should acquire knowledge about the constitution of
the world and of man (that which we now call Theosophy), and that he should develop deep and strong
devotion through worship of the Divine, while he is
striving to awaken the inner layers of Kundalinī and
conduct her (for this force is always spoken of as a
goddess) in a tour through the chakras.

Because all these three objects are in view, we
find in each chakra some symbols which are concerned
with teaching and devotion and need not necessarily
be regarded as constituting any essential or working
part of the chakra. In the services—or collective
yoga practices—of the Liberal Catholic Church we
have a Western example of the same thing. There
also we strive at the same time to stimulate devotion
and to convey spiritual knowledge, while practising
the magic involved in the rites. We must remember
also that in old days the yogis who wandered about

or dwelt in the forests had little recourse even to the written palm-leaf books of those times, and therefore required mnemonic aids, such as many of these symbols give. They sat at times at the feet of their gurus; and they could afterwards remember and recapitulate the Theosophy which they learnt on those occasions with the aid of such notes as are conveyed by these drawings.

THE HEART CHAKRA

It is hardly possible here to attempt a complete explanation of the symbology of all these chakras; it will be sufficient to give an indication of what is probably meant in the case of the heart or Anāhata chakra, of which our figure is an illustration. One of the greatest difficulties in our way is that there are several interpretations of most of these symbols, and that the yogis of India present a front of impenetrable reticence to the inquirer, a stone-wall unwillingness to impart their knowledge or thoughts to any but the student who puts himself *in statu pupillari* with the set purpose of giving himself utterly to the work of Laya Yoga, determined if necessary to spend his whole life at the task in order to achieve success.

This chakra is described in vv. 22-27 of *The Shatchakra Nirūpana*, of which the following is Avalon's summarized translation:

The Heart Lotus is of the colour of the Bandhūka flower [red], and on its twelve petals are the letters *Ka* to *Tha*, with the

Bindu above them, of the colour of vermilion. In its pericarp
is the hexagonal Vāyu-Mandala, of a smoky colour, and above it
Sūrya-Mandala, with the Trikona lustrous as ten million flashes
of lightning within it. Above it the Vāyu Bīja, of a smoky hue,
is seated on a black antelope, four-armed and carrying the goad
(ankusha). In his (Vāyu-Bīja's) lap is three-eyed Īsha. Like
Hamsa (Hamsābha), His two arms are extended in the gestures
of granting boons and dispelling fear. In the pericarp of this
Lotus, seated on a red lotus, is the Shakti Kākinī. She is four-
armed, and carries the noose (Pāsha), the skull (Kapāla) and makes
the boon (Vara) and fear-dispelling (Abhaya) signs. She is of
a golden hue, is dressed in yellow raiment, and wears every variety
of jewel, and a garland of bones. Her heart is softened by nectar.
In the middle of the Trikona is Shiva in the form of a Vāna-Linga,
with the crescent moon and Bindu on his head. He is of a golden
colour. He looks joyous with a rush of desire. Below him is the
Jīvātma like Hamsa. It is like the steady tapering flame of a lamp.

Below the pericarp of this Lotus is the red lotus of eight
petals, with its head upturned. It is in this (red) lotus that there
are the Kalpa Tree, the jewelled altar surmounted by an awning
and decorated by flags and the like, which is the place of mental
worship.[1]

THE PETALS AND LETTERS

The petals of any one of these lotuses, as we
have seen, are made by the primary forces, which
radiate out into the body along the spokes of the
wheel. The number of spokes is determined by the
number of powers belonging to the force which comes
through a particular chakra. In this case we have
twelve petals, and the letters given to these evidently
symbolize a certain section of the total creative power
or life-force coming into the body. The letters
mentioned here are from *Ka* to *Tha*, taken in the regular
order of the Sanskrit alphabet. This alphabet is

[1] *The Serpent Power*, by Arthur Avalon, 2nd edition. Text, p. 64.

extraordinarily scientific—apparently we have nothing like it in Western languages—and its 49 letters are usually arranged in the following tabular form, to which *ksha* is added in order to supply enough letters for the fifty petals of the six chakras.

16 VOWELS
अ a आ ā इ i ई ī उ u ऊ ū ऋ ṛi ॠ ṝi ऌ ḷi ॡ ḹi ए e ऐ ai ओ o औ au · ṁ : ḥ

33 CONSONANTS				
Gutturals	क ka	ख kha	ग ga	घ gha	ङ ṅa
Palatals	च cha	छ chha	ज ja	झ jha	ञ ña
Cerebrals	ट ṭa	ठ ṭha	ड ḍa	ढ ḍha	ण ṇa
Dentals	त ta	थ tha	द da	ध dha	न na
Labials	प pa	फ pha	ब ba	भ bha	म ma
Semi-vowels	य ya	र ra	ळ la	व va	
Sibilants	श śa	ष sha	स sa		
Aspirant	ह ha				

TABLE VI

This alphabet is considered for yoga purposes to include the sum-total of human sounds, to be from the point of view of speech a materially extended expression of the one creative sound or word. Like the sacred word Aum (the sound of which begins in the back of the mouth with *a*, traverses the centre with *u*, and ends upon the lips in *m*) it represents all creative speech, and therefore a set of powers. These are assigned as follows: the sixteen vowels to the throat chakra, *Ka* to *Tha* to the heart, *Da* to *Pha* to the navel, *Ba* to *La* to the second, and *Va* to *Sa* to the first. *Ha* and *Ksha* are given to the Ājnā chakra, and the Sahasrāra Lotus or crown chakra is considered to include the alphabet taken twenty times over.

There is no apparent reason why the letters should have been assigned to the particular chakras mentioned, but there is an increasing number of powers as we ascend the chakras. It is possible that the founders of the Laya system may have had a detailed knowledge of these powers, and may have used the letters to name them much as we use letters in referring to angles in geometry, or to the emanations from radium.

The practice of meditation on these letters has evidently something to do with reaching " the inner sound which kills the outer ", to use a phrase from *The Voice of the Silence*. The scientific meditation of the Hindus begins with concentration upon a pictured object or a sound, and only when the mind has been fixed steadily upon that does the yogi try to pass on to realize its higher significance. Thus in meditating upon a Master he first pictures the physical form, and afterwards tries to feel the emotions of the Master, to understand His thoughts, and so on.

In this matter of sounds the yogi tries to pass inward from the sound as known to us and uttered by us, to the inner quality and power of that sound, and thus it is an aid to the passage of his consciousness from plane to plane. It may be thought that God created the planes by reciting the alphabet and that our spoken word is its lowest spiral. In this form of yoga the aspirant strives by inner absorption or laya to return upon that path and so draw nearer to the Divine. In *Light on the Path* we are exhorted to listen to the song of life, and to try to catch its hidden or higher tones.

The Mandalas

The hexagonal mandala or " circle " which occupies the pericarp of the heart lotus is taken as a symbol of the element air. Each chakra is considered to be especially connected with one of the elements earth, water, fire, air, ether and mind. These elements are to be regarded as states of matter, not elements as we understand them in modern chemistry. They are thus equivalent to the terms solid, liquid, fiery or gaseous, airy and etheric, and are somewhat analogous to our subplanes and planes—physical, astral, mental, etc. These elements are represented by certain *yantras* or diagrams of a symbolic character, which are given as follows in *The Shatchakra Nirūpana*, and are shown within the pericarps of the pictured lotuses.

Sometimes in the following list orange-red is given instead of yellow, blue instead of smoky, and black instead of white in the fifth chakra, though it is explained that black stands for indigo or dark blue.

CHAKRA	ELEMENT	FORM	COLOUR
1	Earth	a square	yellow
2	Water	a crescent moon	white
3	Fire	a triangle	bright red
4	Air	two interlaced triangles (a hexagonal figure)	smoky
5	Ether	a circle	white
6	Mind	...	white

TABLE VII

It may seem curious to the Western reader that the mind should be put among the elements, but that does not appear so to the Hindu, for the mind is regarded by him as but an instrument of consciousness. The Hindu has a way of looking at things from a very high point of view, often apparently from the standpoint of the Monad. For example, in the seventh chapter of the *Gītā*, Shrī Krishna says: " Earth, water, fire, air, ether, manas, buddhi and ahamkāra—these are the eightfold divisions of my manifestation (parkriti)." A little later on He speaks of these eight as " my lower manifestation ".

These elements are associated with the idea of the planes, as before explained, but it does not seem that the chakras are especially connected with them. But certainly as the yogi meditates upon these elements and their associated symbols in each chakra he reminds himself of the scheme of the planes. He may also find this form of meditation a means for raising his centre of consciousness, through the levels of the plane in which it is at the time functioning, to the seventh or highest, and through that to something higher still.

Quite apart from the possibility of going out into a higher plane in full consciousness, we have here a means of raising the consciousness so that it may feel the influences of a superior world and receive impressions from above. The force or influence so received and felt is no doubt the " nectar " of which the books speak, of which we will say more in connection with the raising of the awakened kundalinī to the highest centre.

THE YANTRAS

In *Nature's Finer Forces*[1] Pandit Rāma Prasād presents us with a thoughtful study of the reasons for the geometrical forms of these yantras. His explanations are too lengthy for reproduction here, but we may very briefly summarize some of his main ideas. He argues that just as there exists a luminiferous ether, which is the bearer of light to our eyes, so there is a

[1] *Op. cit.*, p. 2, *et seq*, out of print.

special form of ether for each of the other forms of sensation—smell, taste, touch and hearing. These senses are correlated with the elements represented by the yantras—smell with the solid (square), taste with liquid (crescent), sight with the gaseous (triangle), touch with the airy (hexagon), and hearing with the etheric (circle). The propagation of sound, the Pandit argues, is in the form of a circle, that is of a radiation all around; hence the circle in the fifth chakra. The propagation of light, he says, is in the form of a triangle, for a given point in the light-wave moves a little forwards and also at right angles to the line of progress, so that when it has completed its movement it has performed a triangle; hence the triangle in the third chakra. He argues that there is a movement in the ether also in the cases of touch, taste and smell, and gives reasons for the forms which we find associated with these in their respective chakras.

THE ANIMALS

The antelope, on account of its fleetness of foot, is a suitable symbol for the element air, and the bīja or seed-mantra (that is, the sound in which the power governing this element manifests itself) is given as Yaṁ. This word is sounded as the letter y, followed by the neutral vowel a, (which is like the a in " India "), and a nasal after-sound similar to that which frequently occurs in the French language. It is the dot over the letter which represents this sound, and in that dot is the divinity to be worshipped in this centre—the three-eyed Īsha. Other animals are the elephant, associated with earth on account of its solidity and with ether because of its supporting power; the makara or crocodile in the water of Chakra 2; and the ram (evidently regarded as a fiery or aggressive animal) in Chakra 3. For certain purposes the yogi may imagine himself as seated on these animals and exercising the power which their qualities represent.

THE DIVINITIES

There is a beautiful idea in some of these mantras, which we may illustrate by reference to the well-known sacred word Om. It is said to consist of four parts—a, u, m, and ardhamātrā. There is a reference to this in *The Voice of the Silence,* as follows:

And then thou canst repose between the wings of the Great Bird. Aye, sweet is rest between the wings of that which is not born, nor dies, but is Aum throughout eternal ages.

And Madame Blavatsky in a footnote to this speaks of the Great Bird as

Kāla Hamsa, the bird or swan. Says the *Nādavindu-upanishat* (Rig-veda) translated by the Kumbakonam Theosophical Society—" The syllable A is considered to be the bird Hamsa's right wing, U its left, M its tail, and the Ardhamātrā (half metre) is said to be its head."

The yogi after reaching the third syllable in his meditation, passes on to the fourth, which is the silence which follows. He thinks of the divinity in that silence.

In the different books the deities assigned to the chakras vary. For example *The Shatchakra Nirū-pana* places Brahmā, Vishnu and Shiva in the first, second and third chakras respectively, and different forms of Shiva beyond them, but *The Shiva Samhitā* and some other works mention Ganesha (the elephant-headed son of Shiva) in the first, Brahmā in the second and Vishnu in the third. Apparently differences are made according to the sect of the worshipper.

Along with Īsha in the present instance we have as feminine divinity the Shakti Kākinī. Shakti means power or force. Thought-power is described as a shakti of the mind. In each of the six chakras there is one of these feminine divinities—Dākinī, Rākinī, Lākinī, Kākinī, Shākinī and Hākinī—which are by some identified with the powers governing the various *dhātus* or bodily substances. In this chakra Kākinī is seated on a red lotus. She is spoken of as having four arms (four powers or functions). With two of her hands she makes the same signs of granting boons and dispelling fears as are shown by Īsha; the other two hold a noose (a symbol which is another form of the ankh cross) and a skull (as symbol, no doubt, of the slain lower nature).

THE BODY MEDITATION

Sometimes the meditations usually prescribed for these chakras are assigned to the body as a whole, as in the following extract from *The Yogatattva Upanishad*:

There are five elements, earth, water, fire, air, and ether. For the body of the five elements, there is a fivefold concentration. From the feet to the knees is said to be the region of earth; it is four-sided in shape, yellow in colour and has the letter *La*. Carrying the breath with the letter *La* along the region of earth (from the feet to the knees) and contemplating Brahmā with four faces and of a golden colour, one should perform meditation there. . . .

The region of water is declared to extend from the knees to the anus. The water is semi-lunar in shape and white in colour, and has *Va* for its bīja (seed). Carrying up the breath with the letter *Va* along the region of water, he should meditate upon the god Nārāyana, having four arms and a crowned head, as being of the colour of pure crystal, as dressed in orange cloths and as decayless. . . .

From the anus to the heart is said to be the region of fire. Fire is triangular in shape, of red colour, and has the letter *Ra*, for its bīja or seed. Raising the breath, made resplendent through the letter *Ra*, along the region of fire, he should meditate upon Rudra, who has three eyes, who grants all wishes, who is of the colour of the midday sun, who is smeared all over with holy ashes, and who is of a pleased countenance. . . .

From the heart to the middle of the eyebrows is said to be the region of air. Air is hexangular in shape, black in colour, and shines with the letter *Ya*. Carrying the breath along the region of air, he should meditate upon Īshvara, the omniscient, as possessing faces on all sides. . . .

From the centre of the eyebrows to the top of the head is declared to be the region of ether; it is circular in shape, smoky in colour, and shining with the letter *Ha*. Raising the breath along the region of ether, he should meditate upon Sadāshiva in the following manner—as producing happiness, as of the shape of bindu (a drop), as the Great Deva, as having the shape of ether, as shining like pure crystal, as wearing the rising crescent moon on his head, as having five faces, ten hands and three eyes, as being of a pleasing countenance, as armed with all weapons, as adorned with all ornaments, as having the goddess Umā in one-half of his body, as ready to grant favours, and as the cause of all the causes.

This, to some extent, confirms our suggestion that in some cases the principles upon which we are asked to meditate are applied to parts of the body for purely mnemonic purposes, not with the direct intention of affecting those parts.

THE KNOTS

In the centre of the heart lotus a trikona or inverted triangle is figured. This is not a feature of all the centres, but only of the root, heart and brow chakras. There are in these three special *granthis* or knots, through which kundalinī has to break in the course of her journey. The first is sometimes called the knot of Brahmā; the second that of Vishnu; the third that of Shiva. The idea which this symbolism seems to imply is that the piercing of these chakras in some way involves a special change of state, possibly from the personality to the higher self and thence to the Monad— the regions over which these Aspects may be said to rule. It can, however, be only in a subordinate or secondary manner that this is true, for we have observed that the heart chakra receives impressions from the higher astral, the throat centre from the mental, and so forth. In each triangle the deity is represented as a linga, or instrument of union. The Jīvātmā (literally " living self ") pointing upwards " like the flame of a lamp " is the ego, represented as a steady flame probably because he is not distressed by the accidents of material life, as is the personality.

THE SECONDARY HEART LOTUS

The second small lotus represented as just beneath the heart chakra is also a special feature of this centre. It is used as a place for meditation upon the form of the guru or the Aspect of the Deity which especially appeals or is assigned to the worshipper. Here the devotee imagines an island of gems, containing beautiful trees, and an altar for worship, which is described as follows in *The Gheranda Samhītā*:

Let him contemplate that there is a sea of nectar in his heart; that in the midst of that sea there is an island of precious stones, the very sand of which is pulverized diamonds and rubies. That on all sides of it there are Kadamba trees, laden with sweet flowers; that, next to these trees, like a rampart, there is a row of flowering trees, such as mālatī, mallikā, jātī, kesara, champaka, pārijāta, and padma, and that the fragrance of these flowers is spread all round, in every quarter. In the middle of this garden, let the yogi imagine that there stands a beautiful Kalpa tree, having four branches, representing the four Vedas, and that it is full of flowers and fruits. Insects are humming there and cuckoos singing. Beneath that tree, let him imagine a rich platform of precious gems, and on that a costly throne inlaid with jewels, and that on that throne sits his particular Deity, as taught to him by his Guru. Let him contemplate on the appropriate form, ornaments and vehicle of that Deity.[1]

The worshipper uses his imagination in creating this beautiful scene so vividly as to become enwrapped in his thought and to forget the outer world entirely for the time being. The process is not, however, entirely imaginative, for this is a means to obtain constant contact with the Master. Just as the images of persons made by one who is in the heaven-world after death are filled with life by the egos of those persons, so the Master fills with his real presence the thought-form produced by his pupil. Through that form real inspiration and sometimes instruction may be given. An interesting example of this was presented

[1] *Op. cit.*, VI, 2-8. Trans. Sris Chandra Vidyārnava.

by an old Hindu gentleman who was living as a yogi in a village in the Madras Presidency, who claimed to be a pupil of the Master Morya. When that Master was travelling in Southern India years ago he visited the village where this man lived. The latter became his pupil, and declared that he did not lose his Master after he went away, for he used frequently to appear to him and instruct him through a centre within himself.

The Hindus lay much stress upon the necessity for a Guru or Master, and they reverence him greatly when he is found. They constantly reiterate the statement that he must be treated as divine; *The Tejobindu Upanishad* says: " The furthest limit of all thoughts is the guru." They maintain that were one to think of the glorious qualities of the Divine Being, one's imagination would still fall below the perfections of the Master. We who know the Masters well realize the truth of that; their pupils find in them heights of consciousness splendid and glorious beyond all expectation. It is not that they consider the Master equal to God; but that that portion of the Divine which the Master has attained outshines their previous conceptions of it.

EFFECT OF MEDITATION IN THE HEART

The Shiva Samhitā thus describes the benefits which are said to accrue to the yogi from meditation upon the heart centre:

He gets immeasurable knowledge, knows the past, present and future; has clairaudience, clairvoyance and can walk in the air, whenever he likes.

He sees the adepts, and the goddesses known as Yoginīs; obtains the power known as Khecharī, and conquers the creatures which move in the air.

He who contemplates daily on the hidden *Bānalinga* undoubtedly obtains the psychic powers called Khecharī (moving in the air) and Bhūcharī (going at will all over the world).[1]

It is not necessary to comment upon these poetic descriptions of the various powers; the student will read between the lines. Still, there may also be something in the literal meaning of such statements as these; for there are many wonders in India—the mysterious powers of the fire-walkers, and the perfectly marvellous hypnotic ability shown by some conjurers who perform the famous rope trick and similar feats.

KUNDALINĪ

The Hindu Yogis, for whom the books which have come down to us were written, were not particularly interested in the physiological and anatomical features of the body, but were engaged in practising meditation and arousing kundalinī for the purpose of elevating their consciousness or rising to higher planes. This may be the reason why in the Sanskrit works little or nothing is said about the surface chakras, but much about the centres in the spine and the transit of kundalinī through these.

Kundalinī is described as a devi or goddess luminous as lightning, who lies asleep in the root

[1] *The Shiva Samhitā*, V, 86-88.

chakra, coiled like a serpent three and a half times round the *svayambhu linga* which is there, and closing the entrance to the sushumnā with her head. Nothing is said as to the outer layer of the force being active in all persons, but this fact is indicated in the statement that even as she sleeps she " maintains all breathing creatures ".[1] And she is spoken of as the *Shabda Brahman* in human bodies. *Shabda* means word or sound; we have here, therefore, a reference to the Third Aspect of the Logos. In the process of creation of the world this sound is said to have issued in four stages; probably we should not be far wrong in associating these with our Western conceptions of the three states of body, soul and spirit, and a fourth which is union with the Divine or All-spirit.

THE AWAKENING OF KUNDALINI

The object of the yogis is to arouse the sleeping part of the kundalinī, and then cause her to rise gradually up the sushumnā canal. Various methods are prescribed for this purpose, including the use of the will, peculiar modes of breathing, mantrās, and various postures and movements. *The Shiva Samhitā* describes ten *mudrās* which it declares to be the best for this purpose, most of which involve all these efforts at the same time. In writing of the effect of one of these methods, Avalon describes the awakening of the inner layers of kundalinī as follows:

[1] *The Serpent Power.*

The heat in the body then becomes very powerful, and kundalinī, feeling it, awakens from her sleep, just as a serpent struck by a stick hisses and straightens itself. Then it enters the Sushumnā.[1]

It is said that in some cases kundalinī has been awakened not only by the will, but also by an accident —by a blow or by physical pressure. I heard an example of the kind in Canada. A lady, who knew nothing at all of these matters, fell down the cellar steps in her house. She lay for some time unconscious, and when she awoke she found herself clairvoyant, able to read the thoughts passing in other people's minds, and to see what was going on in every room in the house; and this clairvoyance has remained a permanent possession. One assumes that in this case in falling the lady must have received a blow at the base of the spine exactly in such a position and of such a nature as to shock the kundalinī into partial activity; or of course it may have been some other centre that was thus artificially stimulated.

Sometimes the books recommend meditation upon the chakras without the prior awakening of kundalinī. This appears to be the case in the following verses from *The Garuda Purāna*:

Mūlādhāra, Svādhishthāna, Manipūraka, Anāhatam, Vishuddhi and also Ājnā are spoken of as the six chakras.

One should meditate, in order, in the chakras, on Ganesha, on Vidhi (Brahma), on Vishnu, on Shiva, on Jīva, on Guru, and on Parabrahman, all-pervading.

Having worshipped mentally in all the chakras, with unwavering mind, he should repeat the Ajapā-gāyatrī according to the instructions of the Teacher.

[1] *The Serpent Power.*

He should meditate in the Randhra, with the thousand-petalled lotus inverted, upon the blessed Teacher within the Hamsa, whose lotus-hand frees from fear.

He should regard his body as being washed in the flow of nectar from His feet. Having worshipped in the fivefold way he should prostrate, singing His praise.

Then he should meditate on the kundalini as moving upwards and downwards, as making a tour of the six chakras, placed in three and a half coils.

Then he should meditate on the place called sushumnā, which goes out of the Randhra; thereby he goes to the highest state of Vishnu.[1]

THE ASCENT OF KUNDALINĪ

The books hint at, rather than explain, what happens when kundalini rises up the channel through the sushumnā. They refer to the spine as Merudanda, the rod of Meru, " the central axis of creation ", presumably of the body. In that, they say, there is the channel called sushumnā, within that another called Vajrinī, and within that again a third called Chitrinī, which is " as fine as a spider's thread ". Upon that are threaded the chakras, " like knots on a bamboo rod ".

Kundalini rises up Chitrinī little by little as the yogi uses his will in meditation. In one effort she may not go very far, but in the next she will go a little farther, and so on. When she comes to one of the chakras or lotuses she pierces it, and the flower, which was turned downwards, now turns upwards. When the meditation is over, the candidate leads kundalini

[1] *Op. cit.,* XV, 72, 76, 83-87.

back again by the same path into the Mūlādhāra; but in some cases she is brought back only as far as the heart chakra, and there she enters what is called her chamber.[1] Several of the books say that kundalinī resides in the navel chakra; we have never seen it there in ordinary people, but this statement may refer to those who have roused it before, and so have a sort of deposit of the serpent-fire in the centre.

It is explained that as kundalinī enters and leaves each chakra in the course of her ascent in the above-mentioned variety of meditations she withdraws into latency (hence the term *laya*) the psychological functions of that centre. In each chakra which she enters there is a great enhancement of life, but as her object is to reach the highest she proceeds upwards, until she reaches the topmost centre, the Sahasrāra lotus. Here, as the symbology has it, she enjoys the bliss of union with her lord, Paramashiva; and as she returns on her path she gives back to each chakra its specific faculties, but much enhanced.

All this describes a process of partial trance into which one who meditates deeply necessarily passes, for in concentrating all our attention upon some lofty subject we cease for the time being to pay heed to the various sounds and sights which surround and play upon us. Avalon mentions that it generally takes years from the commencement of the practice to lead the kundalinī into the Sahasrāra, though in exceptional cases it can be done in a short time. With

[1] See *The Voice of the Silence*, Fragment 1.

practice comes facility, so that an expert, it is said, can raise and lower the Shakti within an hour, though he is of course perfectly at liberty to stay as long as he will in the crown centre.

Some writers say that as kundalini rises in the body, the portion beyond which she goes grows cold. No doubt this is the case in those special practices in which a yogi goes into trance for a long period, but not in the usual employment of this power. In *The Secret Doctrine* Madame Blavatsky cites the case of a yogi, who was found on an island near Calcutta, round whose limbs the roots of trees had grown. She adds that he was cut out, and in the endeavour to awaken him so many outrages were inflicted on his body that he died. She mentions also a yogi near Allahabad who—for purposes no doubt well understood by himself—remained sitting upon a stone for fifty-three years. His chelas or disciples washed him in the river every night and then lifted him back, and during the day his consciousness sometimes returned to the physical world, and he would then talk and teach.[1]

THE GOAL OF KUNDALINI

The concluding verses of the *Shatchakra Nirūpana* beautifully describe the conclusion of the tour of kundalini, as follows:

The Devi who is Shuddha-sattva pierces the three Lingas, and, having reached all the lotuses which are known as the Brahmanādi lotuses, shines there in the fullness of her lustre. Thereafter,

[1] *Op. cit.*, Vol. V, p. 544.

in her subtle state, lustrous like lightning and fine like the lotus fibre, She goes to the gleaming flame-like Shiva, the supreme Bliss, and of a sudden produces the bliss of Liberation.

The beautiful Kundalī drinks the excellent red nectar issuing from Para Shiva, and returns from there, where shines Eternal and Transcendent Bliss in all its glory, along the path of Kula, and enters the Mūlādhāra. The yogi who has gained steadiness of mind makes offering (Tarpana) to the Ishta-devatā and the Devatās in the six chakras, Dākinī and others, with that stream of celestial nectar which is in the vessel of Brahmānda, the knowledge whereof he has gained through the tradition of the Gurus.

If the yogi who is devoted to the Lotus Feet of his Guru, with heart unperturbed and concentrated mind, reads this work, which is the supreme source of the knowledge of Liberation and is faultless, pure and most secret, then of a surety his mind dances at the Feet of his Ishta-devatā.[1]

CONCLUSION

Like ourselves, the Hindus hold that the results of Laya Yoga can be attained by the methods of all the systems of yoga. In the seven schools of India, and among the students in the West, all who understand aright are aiming at the highest goal of human endeavour, at that liberty which is higher than liberation, because it includes not only union with God in high realms beyond earthly manifestation, but also those powers on each plane which make the man an Adhikāri Purusha, an office-bearer or worker in the service of the Divine, in the work of lifting the toiling millions of humanity towards the glory and happiness which awaits us all.

OM, AIM, KLĪM, STRĪM

॥ ओं ऐं क्लीं स्त्रीं ॥

[1] *Op. cit.*, vv. 51, 53, 55.

INDEX

QUEST BOOKS
are published by
The Theosophical Society in America,
Wheaton, Illinois 60189-0270,
a branch of a world organization
dedicated to the promotion of the unity of
humanity and the encouragement of the study of
religion, philosophy, and science, to the end that
we may better understand ourselves and our place in
the universe. The Society stands for complete
freedom of individual search and belief.
In the Classics Series well-known
theosophical works are made
available in popular editions.
For more information
write or call.
1-708-668-1571

Other books by Charles W. Leadbeater:

The Astral Plane
Clairvoyance
Dreams
The Inner Life
The Life after Death
Man Visible and Invisible
The Masters and the Path

Available from:
The Theosophical Publishing House
P. O. Box 270, Wheaton, Illinois 60189-0270